A fascinating illustration of traumatogenic processes
defences of encapsulation and social-psychic retreat, t
highly accessible study of the wet nurse, the nanny and
stand the hidden foundling within each of us, especially m
in general and perhaps old-fashioned psychoanalysts in pa   ....acing
the emergence of the relational perspective from the fecund field of attachment
which was originally a matter of dissident and dissonant voices within psychoanalysis, group analysis and sociology, the social unconscious is shown to be
entirely relevant to our understanding of loss and melancholia in the deepest layers
and kernels of our unconscious life.

> **Earl Hopper**, PhD, psychoanalyst, group analyst and editor of
> the New International Library of Group Analysis

Prophecy Coles brings 'delegated' or substitute parents out from obscurity into
the limelight. She explores the many contradictions of this role, asking questions
such as: Can love really be bought? What is the impact on children of losing an
early attachment figure? What does it mean for a child to love someone in a
socially devalued position? What is the cost for the substitute parent herself? I
found this a fascinating and subtly argued book; it deserves to be widely discussed.

> **Sue Gerhardt**, psychotherapist and bestselling author of *Why Love Matters*

The Shadow of the Nurse explores a topic strangely neglected in psychoanalytical
writing. Why have wet nurses and nannies been largely removed from history,
Prophecy Coles asks, even though it is clear from the autobiographical and fictional
writing that their role has been of immense emotional importance to the infants
they have cared for? In her original and wide-ranging study, the author explores
the reasons for this neglect, and on the significance in both past and present of
surrogate forms of maternal care.

> **Michael Rustin**, Professor of Sociology at the University of East London

It has been a great pleasure to read this important contribution to the psychoanalytic
literature on an unfairly neglected theme: the significance and importance of the
nurse and the nanny in infantile early development as well as in childhood in
general. Written with remarkable clarity and concision, the author draws upon a
lifetime of clinical and personal experience and interest in the subject, and in a
series of most elegant chapters that combine literary, social and psychoanalytic
insights, she shares with us her thoughts on the subject. Many are the ideas and
questions this fascinating book presents us with, readily taken by the author with
care, understanding, great intelligence and sensitivity. The book effortlessly
succeeds in transforming 'the shadow of the nurse' in a touching and impressive
presence. This is a most welcome addition to the libraries of everyone with an
interest in children and, as the great Paula Heimann would have said, in 'children-
no-longer'.

> **Luis Rodríguez de la Sierra**, PhD, training and supervising
> adult and child and adolescent psychoanalyst of the
> British Psychoanalytical Society

The Shadow of the Second Mother

The Shadow of the Second Mother explores why there has been such little interest, in psychology, social history and biography, in the important contribution that 'second mothers', such as wet nurses and nannies, have had upon the emotional life of the children they have nursed. For the last 3000 years and throughout most civilisations they have nurtured the children of the privileged, and kept alive the abandoned and unwanted child, and yet there has been a profound silence surrounding the influence they may have had.

The author explores the lives of several well-known people who have been wet nursed, such as Michelangelo, Rousseau, Jack London, Nabokov and Klein. She speculates that they were all affected emotionally by their 'second mother', and concludes that a universal feature of such delegated mothering seems to be that the bond between mother and child is broken, and the child may be left with a lifelong distrust of close relationships. In *The Shadow of the Second Mother*, Coles combines an exploration of attachment theory with neurology, making it possible to give an explanation as to why these important figures have lain unnamed and ignored in our social and psychological consciousness.

This intriguing new approach to an ancient practice will be fascinating reading for psychotherapists, psychoanalysts, sociologists and students of social history.

Prophecy Coles trained at the Lincoln Centre for Psychotherapy, UK, and has had a long association with the London Centre for Psychotherapy. She has worked as a psychotherapist for 30 years and has published widely on the sibling relationship, femininity and transgenerational conflict.

The Shadow of the Second Mother

Nurses and nannies in theories of infant development

Prophecy Coles

Routledge
Taylor & Francis Group

LONDON AND NEW YORK

First published 2015
by Routledge
27 Church Road, Hove, East Sussex, BN3 2FA

And by Routledge
711 Third Avenue, New York, NY 10017

Routledge is an imprint of the Taylor & Francis Group, an informa business

British Library Cataloguing in Publication Data
A catalogue record for this book is available from the British Library

Library of Congress Cataloging-in-Publication Data
Coles, Prophecy.
 The shadow of the second mother: nurses and nannies in theories of infant
 development/Prophecy Coles.
 pages cm
 1. Wet nurses – History. 2. Nannies – History. 3. Mother and child.
 4. Infant development. 5. Infant psychology. I. Title.
 HQ778.5.C65 2015
 649 .1 – dc23
 2014030150

ISBN: 978-0-415-63721-3 (hbk)
ISBN: 978-0-415-63723-7 (pbk)
ISBN: 978-1-315-73989-2 (ebk)

Typeset in Times New Roman and Gill Sans
by Florence Production Ltd, Stoodleigh, Devon, UK

MIX
Paper from
responsible sources
FSC   FSC® C013056
www.fsc.org

Printed and bound in Great Britain by
TJ International Ltd, Padstow, Cornwall

For Michael and Betty

Michael & Joan
with love
Prophecy.
17. May. 2015.

Contents

Acknowledgements

In the first place I have to thank the late Hilary Rubinstein. He made a comment after reading my last book (Coles, 2011) that a chapter I had written on the nurse could be turned into a book. I have taken his advice.

I owe particular thanks to Liane Aukin, Melanie Hart, Earl Hopper, Michael Rustin, Ann Scott, Tanya Stobbs and Jennifer Silverstone, for their thoughtful and insightful editorial comments, their encouragement, and for their generosity in giving up so much of their time to read the emerging manuscript.

I also want to thank Aigli Brouskou, George Constantinidi, Adam Elgar, Sue Gerhardt, Lesley Hall, Katherine Holden, Ravi Menon, Joan Raphael-Leff, Michael and Margaret Rustin and Felicity du Zulueta for their comments and their literary and historical contributions that I have freely used.

As always, my chief thanks go to Walter, for his encouragement and patient reading of innumerable drafts of this book; his support is without measure.

Reference

Coles, P. (2011) *The Uninvited Guest from the Unremembered Past.* London: Karnac.

Introduction

When Odysseus returned home from his 20-year voyage, he was immediately recognised by his wet nurse, Eurycleia, as she bathed his wounded leg. His wife, Penelope, took longer to recognise him (Homer, 1946). Two thousand years later, Freud, writing to his friend Fliess, was trying to recall his nurse. 'I said to myself that if the old woman disappeared from my life so suddenly, it must be possible to demonstrate the impression she made upon me. Where is it then?' (Masson, 1985: p. 271). These two contrasting images of the nurse resonate throughout this book as I explore what I have called 'delegated mothering'. She can be a remembered figure bound up in earliest memories, but, in many cases, she can be no more than a vague 'impression' who lingers tantalisingly out of conscious recall. One result of this vague 'impression' is that she often fails to appear in autobiography, social history, biography and psychological theory, as though her presence has had no meaning.

I have taken the idea that the nurse has lain behind a shadow from Freud's (1917e) paper on *Mourning and Melancholia* in which he contrasts normal mourning with pathological melancholia. Freud states that when some much loved person dies the normal reaction to their loss is to mourn, with all the attendant emotions of 'painful dejection' (p. 244). However there are other cases, when people fall into a state of melancholia, that have many of the same features as mourning, but what is significant is that the person who is mourned is not necessarily dead. The person, as it were, has gone missing, with the result that 'he knows *whom* he has lost but not *what* he has lost' (p. 245). This then leads to the mourner identifying with 'the abandoned object. Thus the shadow of the object fell upon the ego' (p. 248). When Freud laments the difficulty he has in finding 'the impression' of his nurse, he is also intimating that the difficulty may stem from not knowing '*what* he has lost'. This is a situation that can face any child when it loses its nurse and it furthermore suggests that the child may be left with a long lasting melancholia. However what has happened, historically, is that the nurse has been seen as no more than a pale shadow of the mother in the lives of the children she has looked after and any melancholic traces that may have been left when she leaves have been ignored.

In order to try to bring the nurse out of the shadow I have suggested that we should conceptualise her role as one of 'delegated mothering', whether she was a wet nurse or 'dry' nurse or nanny. 'To delegate' is 'to send or commission someone as a deputy or representative, with power to act for another' (*Shorter Oxford English Dictionary*, 1973). This definition covers the point that the wet nurse or nanny has often been 'a deputy' or 'a representative' for the mother and been in sole charge of the care and discipline of the child. In such cases she will have had an important place in the structure of the inner emotional world of the child, and, as the work of Hardin (1985) has shown, she will often be experienced as 'the second mother'.

My interest in the topic of delegated mothering has its foundations in my early life.[1] I had five nannies during the first five years of my life, at the time of the Second World War, yet I could find no 'impression' of them. One result of my failure to find their 'impression' was that it had not occurred to me to be interested in the significance of a nurse or nanny in my clinical work. I worked for 30 years as a psychotherapist but I had no clinical material about nurses. Hanna Segal, who had had a string of nannies during the first six years of her life, commented that she may have suffered 'a depressing streak, not anything damaging' (Hunter, 1993: p. 3). I had also failed to imagine that a nanny or even several nannies may have left a damaging trace, either within myself or in the psychic life of others. My lack of awareness and interest about the possible effect that early relationships with caretakers, other than the mother, might have upon the emotional life of the child, was compounded by the fact that there has been little interest in the nurse or nanny in the psychoanalytic literature, even to this day.[2] This may seem surprising, for, over the last 40 years, there has been an extensive development of interest in the infant mind and this has shifted the emphasis of therapy towards the impact of early relationships.[3] However it seems that the absence of thought about the nurse or nanny in psychoanalytic thinking can in part be attributed to the fact that the earliest relationship is predicated upon the model of the mother and baby, even if in fact she has not looked after the child, and as a result any other caretaker becomes subsumed under the gestalt of the mother (Mahler, 1961).

It was in large part thanks to Valerie Fildes' two books, *Breasts, Bottles and Babies* (1986) and *Wet Nursing: A History from Antiquity to the Present* (1988) that I awoke to the possibility that nurses have played a larger part in the emotional history of child-care than I had imagined. I discovered that behind the child-rearing practices of employing a nanny there lay another world of wet nursing that I knew nothing about. The nanny is little more than an incarnation of the wet nurse, though now she is in a starched apron and a bottle in her hand. In other words, the idealised picture about mothers and mothering, from the early Rennaisance, scarcely matches the historical truth about infant care. This earliest nurse, the wet nurse, has for the last 3000 years kept alive other people's babies by selling 'mother's milk' (Sussman, 1982). Why, Fildes challengingly asked, have 'historians, particularily those in the burgeoning field of women's lives and work, neglected to see wet-nursing as an important job and one which was exclusively female and frequently well paid'? (Fildes, 1988: p. xiii).[4] I discovered that though Freud and Klein employed wet nurses for their children, I found a curious absence of concern in their work about this 'second mother' (Hardin, 1985) and the possible impact she might leave upon the psyche of the child she nurses.

This book is not only concerned with the delegated mothering of the privileged child. Wet nursing was used for the many thousands of unwanted babies who were abandoned at birth. From early Greek and Roman times it has only been through the heroic efforts of wet nurses that unwanted children have been given a chance of survival and, in several cases, these abandoned children have become iconic figures in Western culture. However the literature about abandoned infants and their relationship with their delegated mother scarcely exists. It is more common to find that abandoned children are thought about as an economic burden upon the state, as is shown in the shifting English Poor Laws, and the chief social concern has been to feed them as cheaply as possible (Pinchbeck and Hewitt, 1969). This lack of documentation about the wet nurse and the child who has been abandoned, often because the mother has died, or been too poor to feed it, has meant that I have had to turn to the literary imagination of such writers as Shakespeare (1564–1616) in *Romeo and Juliet,* Charles Dickens (1812–1870) in his novel *Dombey and Son* and George Moore's (1852–1933) novel *Esther Waters*. They all portray some of the emotional conflicts that can beset a wet nurse as well as her own family. I have also relied upon some of the testaments from Coram's Foundling Hospital to fill out the desolate picture of the abandoned child.

More generally, the emotional significance of wet nurses and nannies upon the inner life of the child has still to find its way into most biographies and social histories on child-rearing, though there are a few exceptions (Gaythorne-Hardy, 1993; Fildes, 1986, 1988; Tomlin, 1997). This has meant that I have had to rely upon an imaginative 'speculation' (Edmundson, 1990) as to the psychological impact of these early relationships. I imagined that when Michelangelo (1475–1564) said to Vasari (1511–1574) 'I took the hammer and chisels with which I carve my figures from my wet-nurse's milk' (Nardini, 1990) he really believed that his wet nurse had had a lasting and creative impact upon him. Then I began to discover in the biographies of others who had had wet nurses, that the wet nurse could have a more destructive effect. Talleyrand (1754–1838), who lived with his wet nurse for the first four years of his life, was left permanently lame after she failed to nurse a foot he damaged by falling off a cupboard. This damaged foot seemed to be a good metaphor for the more negative effect a wet nurse could have. Strung between the creative and destructive effects of a wet nurse I learned of another group of children whose wet nurses had been classified as racially inferior, such as the black nurses in the Southern states of the US. Lilian Smith (1897–1966), who was brought up in Georgia and had a black nurse whom she loved more deeply than her mother, found herself torn between the love she had for her nurse and 'the white folk's hell'. This helped me to realise that such a predicament led to a palpable split in the mind of all children with 'two' mothers. In almost all cases the 'second mother' would come from a different culture and embody different values.

However, the validity of turning a psychoanalytic eye upon literary and historical texts raises problems and questions about the social circumstances that have surrounded wet nursing and delegated mothering (Ashplant, 1988).[5] But I have come to the conclusion that texts about the history of child-rearing reveal a constant dialectical tension between those who believed that the employment of wet nurses and nannies was a good thing and those who believed it could disrupt the bonds between parents and their children. This unresolved argument has led me to suggest that one can discern a 'history of emotions' (Burke, 2012) that confronts every parent when a child is born. All parents wonder how best to bring up their child, but in that discussion, two opposing emotional beliefs seem to have always accompanied the debate. There are parents who bring what I have called a 'child-centred approach' in response to the birth of their child; that is to say, they are not anxious that their child will 'devour' all their time and energy. Then there are those who are more apprehensive of the 'devouring' capacity of their child, and so bring an 'adult-centred point of view', which distances them from their child. These two emotionally different responses have dominated child-rearing practices for the last 3000 years[6] and rise above the social conditions of any particular period.[7] This dialectic seems to be confirmed in the continuing debate about appropriate child-care to this day.[8]

I do not want to leave the impression that I believe parents should not have help in bringing up their children. But a more long-term question can be asked – what is the best environment for the child during the earliest years of its life?[9] What I hope to have shown is that if we hand over our child to another to nurture full time, and I want to use the wet nurse as the paradigm of such an encounter, then this relationship can become established in the infant's mind as the centre of security. If this relationship comes to an end too soon or too abruptly there can be a severe trauma in the child's psyche that may lead to a lifelong failure to trust another human being. This is a painful thought and runs against the grain of the demands made upon families today to delegate child-care so that both parents can work.[10] This painful thought, nevertheless, needs to be confronted if we are really to think about the most nurturing early environment for our children. What I also hope to have shown is that if we delegate our child-care to another, this caretaker becomes an important figure not only in the child's life but in our social history. She needs to be remembered, her name recorded and no longer considered as a commodity we can buy in and then discard. Could it be that we have ignored her presence lest her ghost, who has stalked silently through the pages of our social history, confined to a footnote in our emotional life, might tell us something we would not wish to hear?

Notes

1. Steedman (1986) wrote, 'Personal interpretations of past time – the stories that people tell themselves in order to explain how they got to the place they currently

inhabit – are often in deep and ambiguous conflict with the official interpretative devices of a culture' (p. 6). This question was also raised by Coles (2013) in *Being Alongside*. 'How will you look for it, Socrates, when you do not know what it is?' (Plato, *Meno*. 80d.). Coles answered it in the following way. 'I will only see in my data, that which I already think and believe. Thinking through this paradox involves reflecting on what I mean by knowledge, being explicit about my epistemological stance' (p. 11).

2. 'Certainly not all white children experience turmoil and trauma in their relationship with their biological parents, or are surrendered to the primary care of nannies. But this real and powerful cultural phenomenon has not, as I see it, received the attention it deserves, despite its implications for other self-relationships in the broader culture' (White, 2008: pp. 474–5).

3. Exceptionally, Lindner (1954) in *The Fifty Minute Hour* does mention the psychological effect of wet nursing in two twentieth-century cases. In one case, Kirk, who was born in 1918 on the island of Hawaii was immediately handed over to a Hawaiian wet nurse, Myna, who had exclusive care of him. Myna died suddenly when Kirk was six and he was left with a mother who had little interest in him, and then a series of governesses whose care of him was either negligent or abusive. He retreated gradually into a psychotic world in which he lived two lives; one on this earth, where he became a very successful scientist, and one in a world of science fiction. This is an extreme case of the split that can occur in the mind of a child who has two mothers.

4. This view is not entirely accurate; a Google search shows that from the early 1980s feminist historians were researching wet nursing, though the research tended to be directed towards a specified country. This is in contrast to Fildes' research that stretches across the known world. I am grateful to Michael Rustin for pointing this out.

5. Can the psychic structure of the oedipus complex accommodate a second mother? (Ashplant, 2012).

6. See also Gerhardt (2004); McGilchrist (2009).

7. The debate about the 'history of emotion' is reflected in the work of Hodgkin (2012) writing on the autobiography of the seventeenth-century writer, Elizabeth Isham. She said, 'while generic conventions govern its representation' nevertheless, 'childhood emerges as a period of powerful emotions and intense relationship, no less than it is today' (pp. 248–9). Perhaps one of the earliest people to embrace the idea that there were some universal common emotions was Giambattisto Vico (1668–1725), who believed that all cultures were structured around the emotions that were aroused by birth, sexuality and death.

8. See also Alexander (2012); Bergmann (1973); Gedo (1972); Taylor (2012).

9. A recent debate in the *Observer* (12 January 2014) raised the question, 'Is universal childcare in the best interests of our children?' One discussant was of the view that 'plenty of one-year-olds are in 40 hours care' and the implication was that this was without harm to the child. Whereas another speaker quite emphatically stated that 'Certainly long hours need to be legislated against – babies in day care for 40 hours is very concerning.'

10. In the US, there is no universal state maternity leave, though there is a statutory 12-week unpaid maternity leave (en.wikipedia.org.wiki/Maternity_leave_in_the_ United States). In the UK, there is 26 weeks of paid maternity leave and 26 weeks of additional maternity leave. There is also mandatory two-week leave that must be taken after the birth of a baby, although this is extended to four weeks if you work in a factory (www.gov.uk/maternity-pay-leave).

References

Ashplant, T.G. (1988) Psychoanalysis in historical writing. *History Workshop* 26: 102–20.

Ashplant, T.G. (2012) Freud, fin-de-siecle politics, and the making of psychoanalysis. In: *History and Psyche: Culture, Psychoanalysis and the Past*, S. Alexander and B. Taylor (eds). New York: Palgrave Macmillan.

Alexander, S. and Taylor, B. (2012) Introduction. In: *History and Psyche: Culture, Psychoanalysis and the Past*, S. Alexander and B. Taylor (eds). New York: Palgrave Macmillan.

Bergman, M.S. (1973) Limitations of method in psychoanalytic biography. *American Psychoanalytic Association* 21: 833–50.

Bernard, J.F. (1973) *Talleyrand: A Biography*. London: The History Book Club.

Burke, P. (2012). Afterword. In: *History and Psyche: Culture, Psychoanalysis and the Past*, S. Alexander and B. Taylor (eds). New York: Palgrave Macmillan.

Coles, A. (2013) *Being Alongside: For the Teaching and Learning of Mathematics*. Rotterdam; Boston; Taipei: Sense Publications.

Dickens, C. (1848) *Dombey and Son*. London: Thomas Nelson.

Edmundson, M. (1990) *Towards Reading Freud: Self-Creation in Milton, Wordsworth, Emerson and Sigmund Freud*. Chicago; London: The University of Chicago Press.

Fildes, V. (1986). *Breasts, Bottles and Babies*. Edinburgh: Edinburgh University Press.

Fildes, V. (1988). *Wet Nursing: A History from Antiquity to the Present*. Oxford: Basil Blackwell.

Freud, S. (1917e) *Mourning and Melancholia*. S.E.14. London: Hogarth Press.

Gaythorne-Hardy, J. (1993) *The Rise and Fall of the British Nanny*. London: Weidenfeld & Nicolson.

Gedo, J.E. (1972) The methodology of psychoanalytic biography. *American Psychoanalytic Association Journal* 20: 638–49.

Gerhardt, S. (2004) *Why Love Matters: How Affection Shapes a Baby's Brain*. London: Routledge.

Hardin, H.T. (1985) On the vicissitudes of early primary surrogate mothering. *Journal of American Psychoanalytic Association* 33: 609–29.

Hodgkin, K. (2012) Elizabeth Isham's everlasting library: memory and self in early modern autobiography. In: *History and Psyche: Culture, Psychoanalysis and the Past*, S. Alexander and B.Taylor (eds). New York: Palgrave Macmillan.

Homer (1946) *The Odyssey*, E.V. Rieu (trans.). London: Penguin Classics.

Hunter, V. (1993) An interview with Hanna Segal. *Psychoanalytic Review* 80: 1–28.

Lindner, R. (1982) *The Fifty Minute Hour*. New York: The Other Press.

Mahler, M. (1961) Sadness and grief in childhood. *Psychoanalytic Study of the Child* 16: 332–51.

Masson, J.M. (1985) *The Complete Letters of Sigmund Freud to Wilhelm Fliess, 1887–1904*. Cambridge, M.A.; London: Harvard University Press.

McGilchrist, I. (2009) *The Master and his Emissary. The Divided Brain and the Making of the Western World*. New Haven; London: Yale University Press.

Moore, G. (1894) *Esther Waters*. Oxford: Oxford World Classics. 1999.

Nardini, B. (1990) *Michelangelo: Biography of a Genius*, C. Frost (trans.). Florence; Rome: Giunti.

Pinchbeck, I. and Hewitt, M. (1969) *Children in English Society*, Vols 1 & 2. London: Routledge & Kegan Paul.

Shakespeare, W. (1595) [1994] *Romeo and Juliet*. London: Penguin Popular Classics.

Shorter Oxford English Dictionary (1973) Oxford: Oxford University Press.

Smith, L. (1978) *Killers of the Dream*. New York; London: W.W. Norton.

Steedman, C. (1986) *Landscape for a Good Woman*. London: Virago Press.

Sussman, G.D. (1982) *Selling Mother's Milk: The Wet-Nursing Business in France 1715–1914*. Urbana; Chicago; London: University of Illinois Press.

Taylor, B. (2012) Historical subjectivity. In: *History and Psyche: Culture, Psychoanalysis and the Past*, S. Alexander and B. Taylor (eds). New York: Palgrave Macmillan.

Tomlin, C. (1997) *Jane Austen: A Life*. London: Viking.

Vico, G. (1725) [1970] *The New Science*, T.G. Bergin and M.H. Fisch (trans.). London: Cornell University Press.

White, C. (2008) Crossing boundaries: commentary on paper by Sarah Hill. *Psychoanalytic Dialogues* 18: 466–76.

Chapter 1

A brief history of the wet nurse of the privileged[1]

In 1994, the journalist Guiletta Ascoli interviewed 21 Italian men and women about their memories of their *balie*. Ascoli's reason for this project was that she lost her own nursemaid when she was six, at the birth of her sister. The loss of her beloved *balia* left her with a feeling of irreparable pain. The question she then went on to ask was, why did aristocratic and middle-class mothers, like her own, who had no professional employment, hand over their children to wet nurses? Another important question she asked was, what suffering did it cause the wet nurses who had to leave their own babies? There are several points raised by Ascoli's work that will reappear throughout this book. Her work is a striking reminder that wet nursing was still a popular method of feeding infants among the upper classes in parts of Europe and the US up to the beginning of the twentieth century. She brings to our attention that such a method of child-rearing caused great psychological hardship to the infant when the wet nurse left, though this has been largely ignored throughout the centuries. She also draws attention to the fact that wet nursing was especially cruel to the wet nurse, for she was expected to leave her own child and love the child of the rich more than her own.[2]

A brief historical survey of wet nursing shows, as in Fildes' quotation in the chapter title, that it is the oldest profession for women and that it reaches back at least 3000 years. One of the earliest recorded civil contracts was concerned with the employment of a wet nurse in Babylon (c. 1720–1686 BC). It stated that:

> When a man gives his son to a nurse and that son has died in the hand of the nurse, if the nurse has then made a contract for another son without the knowledge of the father and mother, they shall prove it against her and they shall cut off her breast because she has made a contract for another son without the knowledge of his father and mother.
>
> (Fildes, 1988: p. 24)

Wet nursing not only stretches back into Babylonian times but it has been the preferred way of feeding royal infants and the infants of the rich in the Middle East, Mesopotamia and Europe since then. Wet nurses seem not to have been deterred by the threat that their breast might be cut off if their nursling died without proper account, and instead they have profited from selling their milk and often achieved a higher social status as a result of this profession. Some of the earliest records and paintings of wet nurses are to be found in Ancient Eygpt where the nurse was seen as a mother goddess, even though she came from 'the harem of senior officials of the royal palace' (Fildes, 1988: p. 3). An early painting shows Rameses II (c. 1303–1213 BC) being nursed by the goddess Hathor who is given the head of a cow because the cow was seen as the sacred animal.[3] There is also a painting of King Seti (c. 1279–1213 BC), the father of Rameses II, being nursed by the wet nurse the divine goddess Mut, the Queen of all gods. The relationship of the wet nurse to a future Pharoic King was seen to be an intimate and familial one. She was called 'milk sister' to the King, the infant's father, while at the same time because of her divine status, she conferred upon her nursling his right to become the next ruler (Burdin, 2011). These royal wet nurses could call their own children 'milk sisters' to the King (Fildes, 1988: p. 4). So although these wet nurses were slaves in the harem, they achieved an exalted position for themselves and their children and were revered. It is hard today to get our minds around the fact that it was believed that the power of a future ruler, in early Egyptian civilisation, was bestowed by the divine status of his wet nurse. But perhaps we need to re-evaluate this ancient reverence for the lactating mother and the belief in the lifesaving quality of her milk.[4]

The reverence the wet nurse was given rested on the practical knowledge that her milk protected the infant and enhanced its chances of survival. There was no good alternative to human milk, though drinking feeders are to be found from the earliest civilisations (Fildes, 1986). This practical knowledge that human milk was the best food to ensure the infant's survival did not rest upon the belief that the milk necessarily had to be that of its mother. It needed to be 'mother's milk' and this could be provided by anyone who had recently had a child; in other words it could be the milk of a wet nurse.[5]

The divine status of the wet nurse gradually declined though not the efficacy of 'mother's milk', nor was there a decline in the belief that wet nursing was the best way to ensure the life of a royal infant. Royal households across the world employed wet nurses for the royal infants up until the twentieth century, though the way these wet nurses were treated or thought about varied from country to country. For instance, a particular reverence was given to the wet nurses of the Spanish royal family from the twelfth century onwards. It has been suggested that the treatment of the Spanish wet nurse may have been influenced by the status wet nurses were given by the Muslim religion as it spread across Spain and influenced medieval thinking (Fildes, 1988). Mohammed was orphaned at birth (530 AD) but his life was saved by his wet nurse Halima. Unique rules concerning the relationship between the wet nurse and her nursling were then laid out in the Koran. It was believed that the wet nurse became the 'milk mother' of the child she fed, and this tie of milk joined her with the blood line of the whole family of the nursed child. She and her husband were seen as 'milk-kin' and therefore strict rules of consanguinity were drawn up. No child who had been fed by a wet nurse could marry into her family and these rules exist into the present day in Arab countries (Fildes, 1988).[6] Nowhere else has there been such explicit recognition of the sexual bonds that are created between the wet nurse and child, and in this recognition there is a profound insight into an aspect of the psychology of wet nursing.

In the Spanish royal families, in spite of the possible influence of the Muslim faith, such rules of consanguinity were not drawn up within the Christian faith. Nevertheless, the Spanish wet nurse was given great respect and when her work came to an end she would be given, with her husband, a property so that they could both live out their days of retirement in some economic security.[7] In France, the wet nurse of a royal nursling might be high born herself and would therefore already be treated with respect and be seen as equal to the royal baby in status. On the cover of Fildes' (1988) book on wet nursing, there is a portrait of Louis XIV in the arms of his wet nurse, who is a noblewoman, Marie de Longuet de la Giraudiere.[8]

The wet nurses of the English royal families remain more hidden and are for the most part unnamed in biographies. The three Tudor babies of Henry VIII, Mary, Elizabeth and Edward VI, all had wet nurses, and though the search for a good wet nurse was undoubtledly of prime consideration, the wet nurses disappear anonymously into the nursery household where they might live alongside the head nurse, the rocker and an under nurse (Castor, 2010).[9] Queen Victoria used wet nurses for all her nine children but only two wet nurses have a name, and this was because of the notoriety of one, not because of the intrinsic value that was placed upon her. Queen Victoria employed Mary Ann Brough as a wet nurse for the Prince of Wales in 1841. Brough's husband worked on the estate of Osborne and she had had six children when she was taken into the royal household. Whether she fed any of Victoria's five children who followed is not clear. However, when Prince Leopold was born in 1853, he was sickly, with haemophilia it was later discovered, and his first wet nurse, Mrs MacIntosh, was dismissed as he was not thriving. Brough was brought back and fed him for a year. Why we know her name is that there was a notorious scandal about her when she left the royal household in 1854. She murdered her six children, because, it was said, her husband wanted to divorce her and take them away. She was deemed to be mad and was imprisoned for the rest of her life. Queen Victoria was disturbed by this event and the possible influence Brough might have had upon her children. For instance it was well known that she had a difficult relationship with her eldest son, the Prince of Wales, who had been fed by Brough. She thought Bertie was stupid and slow. Did she fear that these characteristics were due to the influence that Brough's milk had had upon him? (Longford, 1964; www.murderpedia.org).[10]

It can be seen that the practice of using wet nurses for English royal children was still flourishing into the late nineteenth century, but we do not know whether these wet nurses were pensioned off into more comfortable circumstances when they retired, as in Spain. Whatever was the lot of these royal wet nurses, Fildes suggests that the practice of employing wet nurses for royal children arose partly from custom and partly from ritual. But in view of the fact that we seldom learn the names of these women, or have records of what happened to them, it would seem that behind the custom and ritual of wet nursing, there may have been a social belief that all things surrounding the royal breast needed to be hidden and kept in shape.

The belief in the efficacy of wet nursing spread to the aristocratic and rich middle classes in most societies from the period of Classical Greece until the late eighteenth century (Fildes, 1988).[11] A nice example in Greece concerns the employment of a wet nurse for Plutarch's (46–120 AD) daughter Timoxena. This wet nurse would have been a slave, although it is clear she was much loved and respected. Timoxena died when she was two and Plutarch, who was abroad at the time, wrote his wife a heartbreaking letter. He remembers the relationship his daughter had with her wet nurse.

> She used to encourage her wet-nurse to offer and present her breast not only to other babies, but also to her favourite playthings and toys: she was unselfishly trying to share the good things she had and the things she most enjoyed with her favourites, as if they were guests at her very own table.
>
> (Plutarch, 2008: p. 2)

This delightful picture of the wet nurse who seems to be part of a large and loving family is also found in the literature of Homeric Greece. Odysseus' wet nurse is still living in his home when he returns from his 20-year voyage, and she recognises him before his wife, Penelope (Homer, 1946). Orestes' wet nurse is part of Clytemnestra's household and makes a brief appearance, weeping, as she imagines Orestes, 'my heart's care', might be dead (Aeschylus, 1928: l. 742).[12] In such households the wet nurse would be given a high status and would supervise the other servants, and if her nursling was a girl, the wet nurse might accompany her into her new home when the girl married (Fildes, 1988).

By the time of the Roman Empire (300 BC–400 AD), the picture of the wet nurse shifts slightly. She was, like the Greek wet nurses, a slave and would be part of a Roman household in which wealthy Roman women seldom fed their own babies. The wet nurse, when she had given birth, often to her master's child, would be expected to hand her own child over to another wet nurse, while her milk was sold to a Roman family at a higher price. In other words there was a trade in the milk of wet nurses within some Roman families. Alternatively she might be expected to feed an abandoned infant whom her master had bought at the *lactaria* in the local town.[13] This method of buying an unwanted baby was a cheap way in which a rich Roman could expand his household of slaves. These Roman wet nurses seemed no more than a milk commodity, though they would have a higher status than other slaves and might on occasions be able to gain their freedom. This cultural disregard for the wet nurse seems to have spread over the centuries and was to be found in Renaissance Italy. In Florence she might be a Tartar slave and have the status of a commodity that all rich Florentines needed to possess. At the same time she might be used to serve the sexual needs of her master, and possibly his unmarried sons. She might also be loaned out to friends where she would be used for 'nursing their newborn children'. In the case of her own child, it would be sent to the local foundling hospital (Klapisch-Zuber, 1987: pp. 140–1).

One of the difficulties that one confronts when reading about the history of wet-nursing is to know how extensive it was. Fildes neither claims that wet nursing was ubiquitous among the rich, nor does she deny its existence. Instead she writes that 'many wealthy and noble families employed wet nurses to feed their children whilst in poorer families the mother nursed her own child' (1988: p. 34). She nevertheless qualified her account with the comment that there were fluctuating patterns of wet nursing from the Middle Ages until the late nineteenth century. For instance, in Renaissance Florence most Florentine babies were sent out to wet nurses; and a similar pattern was to be found across France, even into the nineteenth century, where wet nursing was used not only by the rich but by the artisans working in shops and factories.[14] The belief that wet nursing was extensive especially within the families of the aristocratic and middle-class families in Europe was endorsed by deMause (1976) who wrote, 'the average child of wealthy parents spent his earliest years in the home of a wet-nurse, returned home to the care of other servants, and was sent out to service, apprenticeship or school by age seven' (p. 32). There are others who claim that the wet nurse was used more extensively by the rich middle class in Catholic countries such as France and Italy. Underlying this claim there is a suggestion that Catholicism helped to support the practice of wet nursing because of its rules about sexual intercourse and procreation.[15] Then there are others who are sceptical about wet nursing altogether and believe that, 'Most women in the early middle period [1500–1800] breast-fed their own children, something we would never guess from the tirades against wet-nursing that began in the late seventeenth century and continued through the eighteenth' (Hufton, 1995: p. 191). Such a view has been corroborated by Heywood (2001), who wrote,

> The consensus among historians is that most mothers in the past breastfed their own children. Wet nursing was after all confined to the larger, older cities of the West, and correspondingly rare in villages, small towns and new industrial centres in the nineteenth century.
>
> (p. 69)

There have been others who have written even more emphatically that, 'all but a small minority of the noble and prosperous . . . could afford wet nurses . . . the nursing mother represented the ideal . . . she was also to a very large extent the reality' (McLaughlin, 1976: p.115). Finally, there have been those who, when writing about English family life, make no reference to wet nursing at all as though it did not exist, or if it did, it had no social or psychological significance to the dynamics of the family or the life of women (see Mate, 1996). One example of such a view comes from Anthony Fletcher (2008), who when writing about growing up in England between 1600 and 1914 suggested that there were no 'grounds for supposing that anything of fundamental importance changed between 1600 and 1914 in the dynamic of the relationships between English parents and their children' (p. xxi).

Dorothy Leigh, writing *The Mothers Blessing* in the seventeenth century, believed that every mother should feed her child at her breast, with the exhortation, 'will shee not blesse it euery time it suckes on her brests, when shee feeleth the bloud come from her heart to nourish it?' (Brown, 1999: p. vi). Whereas Leigh's exact contemporary, Elizabeth Joscelin, in her manuscript, *Mother's Legacy,* published after her death in 1624, expected to find a wet nurse for her own child, 'a religious nurse no matter for her complexion as near as may be chuse a house wheare it may not learn to swear or speak scurrilos words' (Brown, 1999: p. 107). These conflicting points of view are to be found throughout the history of wet nursing and were being disputed into the late eighteenth and early nineteenth centuries. The Duchess of Devonshire (1757–1806) insisted upon breast feeding her three legitimate children for several months, but this behaviour not only shocked her mother and her contemporaries but was thought worthy of an ironical comment in the *The Morning Post*: '[It is remarkable] that females in high life should generally be such strangers to the duty of a mother, as to render one instance to the contrary so singular' (Foreman, 1998: p. 122).

In spite of the arguments that range around the extent of wet nursing, support for its practice can only be understood against the backdrop of the popular medical superstitions that held sway from the first century AD across the Mediterranean world until the eighteenth century. The most influential medical authority in pre-industrial Europe was Soranus of Ephesus (98–117 AD). In his text *Gynnecology* he wrote that 'maternal milk is in most cases unwholesome' (Fildes, 1986: p. 90). The reason for this belief stemmed from the fear that colostrum was poisonous to the newborn infant because it was 'thick, too caseuous and therefore hard to digest' (Fildes, 1986: p. 91) so the baby must not be fed by the mother until her milk had come in on the third day, and since it was obvious that babies needed to be fed if they were to survive these first three days, a wet nurse was needed.

It was not only the fear that colostrum might poison the newborn infant; there were also other ingrained anxieties that surrounded menstrual blood, pregnancy and breast milk. Aristotle (384–322 BC) in his *Historia Animalium* suggested that 'Women continue to have milk until their next conception. . . . so long as there is a flow of milk the menstrual purgations do not take place.' This was an accurate observation that was borne out by the fact that a woman's fertility was diminished if she breast fed, and breast fed on demand. However, then he goes on to express a superstitious dread that if a woman becomes pregnant during the time she is feeding her baby then 'the milk is found, . . . [to be] unfit for use' (Fildes, 1988: p. 9). And why the milk is unfit is that 'the menstrual purgations' must have taken place and menstrual blood will have contaminated her milk.

These fears were still being expressed in the Rennaissance; Leonardo da Vinci (1452–1519) asserted that menstruation 'never happens to good nurses . . . [in whom] all the blood which is retained is dedicated to the nourishment of the infant'; and to support such a belief there were medieval and Renaissance anatomy texts that showed a duct leading from the uterus to the breast (Fildes, 1986: p. 181).[16] Alongside these superstitious beliefs about menstruation and breast milk, Soranus also encouraged women to employ a wet nurse 'lest the woman grow prematurely old, having spent herself through the daily sucking' (Fildes, 1986: p. 16). So Soranus' medical authority helped to reinforce the anxiety about breast milk and sexuality as well as to support the vanity of rich women, who may not have wished to become 'prematurely old' by suckling their child.

Soranus' medical text, *Gynaecology,* found endorsement within the Christian beliefs that were beginning to take hold by the seventh century AD. The Catholic doctrine upheld a belief that sex should be for procreation and therefore a wife must 'provide for the frailty of her husband by paying the conjugal due' (Fildes, 1986: p. 105). How was she to do that and feed a baby? If she was to become pregnant then her milk would be poisonous to her baby, but yet the Christian doctrine expected her to give her husband his 'conjugal dues'. Could she make him wait two years, the expected length of time that a baby should be breast fed? One solution to this difficulty was that rich middle-class men put pressure upon their wives to employ a wet nurse so that they (the husbands) could indulge in as much sex as they pleased. As Mary Wollstonecraft (1759–1797) pertinently wrote, 'There are many husbands so devoid of sense and parental affection that, during the first effervescence of voluptuous fondness, they refuse to let their wives suckle their children' (Stone, 1990: p. 270).

At the same time as the superstitious fears about sexuality, menstruation and breast milk helped to sustain the custom of hiring a wet nurse, across the centuries, there grew up another practice that supported wet nursing. There was a mistaken belief that 'farming out' (Boswell, 1988) children to wet nurses in the country might ensure their survival. This was at a time when infant mortality was extremely high throughout Europe. At the beginning of the eighteenth century in England, one in three babies died before the age of two and only one in two survived to the age of 15 (Pugh, 2007). In London, nearly 50 per cent of children born between 1730 and 1779 did not survive to their fifth birthday (Pinchbeck and Hewitt, 1969). An important reason for this high infant mortality rate, Fildes (1986) argued, could be attributed to the superstition that colostrum damaged the infant. In fact colostrum is essential because it helps the infant build up resistance to bacterial diseases, principally in the gut. Furthermore the newborn infant will have built up a 'measure of immunity' both in utero and within 'the mother's immediate environment' against infection (Fildes, 1986: p. 200). So the infant, who was taken away from the environment that would have given it some protection from infection, and who was sent, often over several days, to a new environment, would have been subjected to a host of new micro-organisms. This medical ignorance about the benefits of colostrum was compounded by little understanding about disease or hygiene. It was observed by Dr Stephen Hales (1756) that if 'the smoky air of the City, [is] so avowedly contrary to the rearing of animals, as well as vegetables', it might be contrary to rearing infants as well (Fildes, 1988: p. 163). So, on the evidence that animals and vegetables did not grow well in the dirt and smells of the city, it seemed quite reasonable, if one had the money, to send one's child to a wet nurse in the country, where it would remain for two or three years, until weaned.

Another reason for employing wet nurses, it has also been suggested, was that their use had the psychological benefit of distancing parents from the possible devastation they would experience if their infant died (Stone, 1990).This view seems to have been embodied in the belief that it was better for parents not to become too attached to their child until it had managed to survive the first two or three years of life. This detachment had, however, one unwelcome consequence. Sending a child away into the country to a wet nurse broke the bond between infant and parent and in many cases that bond was never restored.[17] In 1770 Mrs Thrale had a premature daughter who was not expected to live, and Mrs Thrale's comment was 'she is so very poor a creature I can scarce bear to look on her' (Stone, 1990: p. 57). We can sense she was steeling herself against the possible pain of the death of this daughter, who in fact did live into old age, though she and her mother never got on well together (Hyde, 1977).

The high infant mortality rate must have caused extreme anguish to fathers and mothers alike and yet the middle-class remedy of sending a child away for several years to a wet nurse also inflicted severe emotional pain upon many parents. It is impossible not to feel anguished when reading Mary Verney's words to the steward who was taking her son Ralph with his wet nurse to the country in 1647, 'the child will nott endure to be long out of ones armes' (Fildes, 1988: p. 82). So, paradoxically, many well meaning and loving parents sent their infants into the healthier country air, where it was hoped they would have a greater chance of survival, yet at these partings the parents could suffer almost as much anguish as if their child had died and the child in the future would have to struggle to come to terms with having 'two mothers' (Hardin, 1985).

It was not until the eighteenth century that figures about the extent of infant mortality began to be collected. These figures revealed that 'farming out' one's child did not ensure its survival. However this knowledge seems to have been disregarded altogether in such countries as France. One finds that between 1770 and 1776, the Bureau of Wet Nurses in Paris placed approximately 66,000 babies to wet nurses in the country and this was in a population in Paris that stood between half a million and a million inhabitants (Damroch, 2007). Yet, 30 per cent of these 'farmed out' babies died whereas, between 1774 and 1794, of those who were nursed at home, only 18 per cent died (Sussman, 1982: p. 65). The practice nevertheless continued in France. As late as 1867 Dr Andre-Theodore Brochard, writing about infants in Bordeaux, commented that,

> Most of the women in Bordeaux do not nurse themselves . . . Each year the customs administration . . . can say how many bottles of wine . . . entered Bordeaux . . . But no one can say how many newborns from this city were sent out to nurse, how many are living, how many are dead.
>
> (Fildes, 1988: p. 106)

Whereas in England by the late nineteenth century the practice of 'farming out' babies was almost abandoned. This decline in England was helped by two factors. Louis Pasteur's scientific discoveries about disease and cleanliness led to the pasteurisation of animal milks. This was followed in 1869 by a bottle that was invented and called in the *Medical Times and Gazette* 'The Mamma', an 'infant's feeding bottle' that was 'an admirable and healthful substitute for Nature's Nursing' (Fildes, 1988: p. 202).

Alhough the collection of statistics and death rates helped to bring about some change in thinking about the efficacy of 'farming out' one's child to a wet nurse, there was another significant shift that altered the pattern of infant feeding and helped to bring about the end of the practice of employing a wet nurse. There had begun at the Enlightenment a slow questioning about the superstitious beliefs about breast milk, menstruation and sexuality. A new belief in the value of observation and reason began to take hold and one result was that scientific and medical knowledge gained a firmer footing (Holmes, 2009). One nice example that helped to bring about a change in the belief that colostrum damaged the health of the newborn infant was the observation of William Hunter (1718–1783), who worked in a Lying-In Hospital in London. There was a high incidence of milk fever among the mothers, who were being forbidden to feed their infants for the first two or three days of the infant's life. He recommended that the mothers should breast feed their babies straight away and the incidence of milk fever almost disappeared, and alongside this practical observation the mortality of both mother and infant decreased (Fildes, 1986). Hunter's observation, that mother and baby survived better if the baby was fed at birth, important though it was, took time to be assimilated and so his observation did little to diminish the employment of wet nurses until the late nineteenth century and early twentieth century.

In the discussion so far, of some of the medical, psychological and cultural beliefs that have underpinned the worldwide use of the wet nurse, there needs to be added Shorter's (1977) almost mystical view that the habit of wet nursing suited both the rich and the poor. The rich were able to engage in sexual intercourse and have more children, which they much desired at a time when infant mortality was high, and the poor were able to limit their fertility, by breast feeding another's child, and their monetary gain benefited their impoverished circumstances.

In spite of Shorter's mystical view about the way wet nursing suited both rich and poor, and the more extensive superstitious beliefs about the relationship between sexuality, menstruation and breast milk, which underpinned the employment of wet nurses, their employment was not as straightforward as it might seem. By the first century AD there were rules and contracts being drawn up about the length of time a wet nurse should be employed and also there began to be advice as to the type of woman who was suitable for a wet nurse. Soranus of Ephesus (98–138 AD), who, as has been seen, had much to say on breast feeding, also had strong views about the choice of a wet nurse. She should be between the ages of 25 and 40; she needed to have had two or three children; the sex of her latest infant should be a son of about two months old and her milk needed to be thick and sweet smelling. She also needed to have a good and calm temperament and she certainly must not be a redhead with freckles! What seems to underlie these rules was an intuitive appreciation that the wet nurse may be having an effect upon the child she nurses. Some of the characteristics of the wet nurse that Soranus recommended were clearly sound and the belief that she should be of a calm and reasonable temperament reflected the intuitive knowedge that her mental state will be mirrored by her child, a belief that is current to this day (Gerhardt, 2004).

These rules and contracts about the employment of the wet nurse reflected other anxieties. The knowledge that the wet nurse was usually of a different class and had a different lifestyle to those who employed her meant that one could never be sure one had chosen the best wet nurse, especially if the infant was to die, as the civil contract in Babylon suggested. This anxiety was reflected in the rules and regulations that hedged around the nurse's employment. It was believed that the wet nurse, like the natural mother, must abstain from sexual intercourse, for what held true for all women was that menstruation, pregnancy and sexual inter-course might harm the child she was nursing. In the sixteenth century in England there are records expressing the anxiety that the milk of a pregnant wet nurse could kill the infant she was suckling. 'She gave "pregnant" milk to my daughter for a month and [the baby] nearly died of it' (Fildes, 1988: p. 58).

These regulations, which were so passionately believed to be true, obscured the idea that the state of the baby's health might contribute to its survival. When Samuel Johnson (1709–1784) was born he was sent out to a wet nurse but he was weaned and taken away from her when he was only two and half months old. The reason that Johnson was taken away prematurely from his wet nurse was that he developed an 'inflammation' on his buttocks which became 'scrofulous sores' afflicting every part of his body. The family doctor told his mother that his sores were the result of 'the bad humours of the nurse' and he was taken home 'a poor, diseased infant, almost blind' (Nokes, 2009: pp. 6–7). However Fildes (1986) gives a very different account. She says that Johnson's wet nurse had successfully fed her own son for 18 months and he had shown no signs of ill health. Furthermore the research of McHenry and Mackeith (1966) on Johnson's childhood illnesses exonerates his wet nurse from blame.

It was of course not unreasonable to be concerned for one's infant's welfare, and in the absence of medical observation, and the high incidence of infant mortality, it was not surprising that the death of one's child when in the care of a wet nurse could be attributed to either the quality of her milk or to her negligence or to her state of health. John Evelyn (1620–1706) writing in his diary lamented the fact that his son Richard, aged one month, had died while being 'farmed out' to a wet nurse. He commented that 'we suspected much the nurse had overlain him' (Fildes, 1986: p. 196). The idea that a wet nurse might suffocate her nursling, by lying on him, was a common anxiety that was attributed to the sudden death of an otherwise healthy child, such as Evelyn's son Richard. Fildes (1986) suggests that many of these sudden deaths were probably what today are called 'cot deaths'.

In spite of all these anxieties about the wet nurse, what helped to sustain the practice was the belief that the milk from animals could turn infants into coarse brutes. For instance, goat's milk would send the infant 'goatish' (Fildes, 1986: p.73) or sheep's milk would make the child stupid. Gerald Brenan (1894–1987) was fed as an infant by a goat who had recently given birth. This goat and kid went everywhere with Brenan and his parents even when they returned from Malta to England. Gaythorne-Hardy (1993), wondering about the effect that being fed by a goat might have had upon Brenan, wrote, 'When I visited him in his new house in 1971 he was busy planting his garden, though not with flowers. He was planting thistles' (p. 148). So the superstition lives on!

The recognition that employing a wet nurse could not guarantee the survival of the infant she nursed did bring up other questions, such as, was it natural for mothers to put their babies in the arms of another? Or what effect did it have upon the bond between parent and child? This concern was reflected in books that were much more philosophical and psychological in their approach to infant care than the medical writings of Soranus, who was writing on infant feeding. Aulus Gellius (130–180), a contempory of Tacitus and Pliny in the second century AD, suggested that the wet nurse came between the mother and child and he reprimanded those mothers who allowed their children to be fed by a wet nurse.

> For when a child is removed from its mother and given to a stranger, the energy of maternal fondness by little and little is checked, and all the vehemence of impatient solicitude is put to silence. And it becomes much more easy to forget a child which is put out to nurse, than one of which death has deprived us. Moreover, the natural affection of a child, its fondness, its familiarity, is directed to that object only from which it receives its nourishment, and thence . . . the child has no knowledge of its mother, and no regret for the loss of her.
> (Gellius, 2012: p. 326)

But Gellius' exhortation seems to have been ignored by many.

On 28 February 1533 Michel Montaigne was born on his family estate between Bordeaux and Perigord and he was immediately 'farmed out' to a peasant wet nurse in the region of Perigord. He lived with this family until he was weaned, probably at two years of age as was the custom. Michel's father Pierre wanted his son to learn of the peasant way of life so that when he came to run the family estate he would understand his servants. What better way of doing that than by imbibing a peasant's breast milk? When Montaigne was returned to his family he never felt close to his mother, and she seems never to have liked him much and found him lazy and idle (Bakewell, 2011). However one successful outcome of Montaigne's early years of peasant life was that he was revered by the peasants he employed on his estate and he was particularly kind to animals.

There were other tensions that surrounded the debate about wet nursing. These were exemplified by religious regulations that were being drawn up across Europe, from the twelth century onwards, stating who could or who could not become a wet nurse. For instance, Christians were instructed not to feed Muslim or Jewish infants; Muslims considered that Christian wet nurses were unsuitable, and Jewish women should not wet nurse Christian children. In some Jewish communities non-Jewish women were employed as wet nurses though they were closely supervised to see that the infants were not being given 'unclean' food. In the seventeenth century religious regulations still continued and Protestants would not employ Catholic wet nurses and vice versa (Fildes, 1988).

Finally there was a fear that the wet nurse might swap the nursling with her own baby when it was returned home to its parents. This was a quite imaginable anxiety for parents who 'farmed out' their child for two or three years and never visited it during this time. This anxiety tends to be expressed either in fiction or in anecdote. Luigi Tansillo, a sixteenth century poet, wrote about such abuse, 'Strange is the tale, but not more strange than true, / And many a parent may the treachery rue, / Who for the child, neglected and unknown, / Receive a changeling, vainly deemed their own' (Fildes, 1988: p. 78). Another example that runs through a particular family history to this day, is the fear that there may be 'foreign' blood in the family. In 1822 the Turks invaded the Greek island of Chios. One prosperous Greek family had a Turkish wet nurse for their son; at the height of the invasion the wet nurse fled to the safety of the mountains with her nursling and her own child and hid them both in a well. She returned with the children when the danger had died down, but ever since the Greek family, in jocular moments, wondered whether the child she returned was in fact their Greek son or her own. In other words, is there Turkish blood in this Greek family?[18]

By the eighteenth century another question about wet nursing was beginning to be asked; was it natural for a wet nurse to give up her own child in order to feed a more privileged child? This was in contrast to the popular attitude that had been exemplified in Renaissance Florence. 'Florentines were insensitive to the moral handicap that weighed on their [wet] nurses – women who had to give up raising their own children' (Klapisch-Zuber, 1987: p. 140). It was a significant shift in emotional and social imagination when for the first time there was some consideration for the wet nurse and the suffering that was caused when she was expected to give up her own child. There are no written records from the wet nurse or her child, if it survived, for she was usually illiterate, but this idea begins to be expressed in literature. There are two nineteenth-century fictional accounts of wet nurses, Polly in *Dombey and Son* (Dickens, 1848) and Esther in *Esther Waters* (Moore, 1894). Polly and Esther are both expected to ignore their maternal feelings for their own children and leave them while they lived in the home of the more privileged child. The moral implication that underpins the writing of both these works is that a wrong is being done to these women and their own child. This conflict for the wet nurse had not been so brutal in earlier centuries when the nursling was 'farmed out' to the wet nurse's home and her own child lived alongside this new baby. In these circumstances and far from the inconstant supervision of her employers or supervisors the strict rules that were laid out were seldom followed and she may well have fed both babies at the same time, if she was able (Fildes, 1988).

Nevertheless it can be safely said that wet nursing must have caused suffering to both the wet nurse and her own child if they were separated. But what was the experience of the privileged middle-class infant that she looked after? Did it also suffer? The 'farmed out' infant, between the seventeenth and late nineteenth centuries, in England, might have been sent 40 miles away from its home, usually immediately after birth, and would have seldom been visited by its parents, for journeying was a hazardous business until roads became tarmacked in the nineteenth century. And however loving and kind the wet nurse might have been, and most of the evidence suggests she usually was, for otherwise she would not find further employment (Fildes, 1988), the 'farmed out' infant would have to make at least two adjustments during the first two or three years of its life. It would have no sooner become familiar with a rural way of life and community than it would have had to readjust to an urban world on its return to its parents. In many cases the infant may have had more than one wet nurse before it was returned to its mother.[19] Whether the nursling had only one wet nurse or more than one, it is safe to conclude that there would have been pain and hardship as the infant had to adapt to at least two environments. Talleyrand (1754–1838), writing of his experiences of being 'farmed out' to a wet nurse for the first four years of his life, wryly commented that 'These first disappointments of my life taught me to bear misfortune and disappointment with indifference and to meet such things with the resources which my self knowledge taught me I possessed' (Bernard, 1973: p. 29). 'Indifference' may well have been the best word to describe the protective armour some children would have had to put on as they negotiated their emotional life.

There were, however, other very different accounts from nurslings when they left their wet nurses. In the fourth century BC a Greek epitaph reads, 'Here Hippostrate still misses you. I loved you while you were alive, nurse, I love you still' (Fildes, 1988: p. 10). An equally distressing note was written by Pierre Coustel in 1687 as he tried to find a way to integrate his love for his wet nurse and his anger with his mother.

> I show more affection and gratitude to the one to whom I owe the most. When the time for your lying in came you rid yourself of me as a burden that was inconvenient . . . while instead my nurse continually caressed me, nourished me for two years with her own milk and by her care and trouble brought me to the vigorous manhood in which you see me at present.
>
> (quoted in Marvick, 1976: p. 268)

It is important not to forget that there was another hardship occasioned by wet nursing. The wet nurse herself may well have suffered when she returned her nursling to its parents but there would have been little conscious recognition from her employers that a bond would have been created between herself and the child or that its severance might be painful for her. A letter written by a wet nurse in France in 1785 could surely have been echoed by many others. She had nursed a little boy for two years before he was returned to his family. She wrote to his parents soon after his return, and put her feelings into the words of her daughter. 'It seems very strange to me not to see him anymore . . . My little girl asks me every day for him, the little brother' (Sussman, 1982: p. 78).

This brief outline on the history of the wet nurse of the privileged shows a social and psychological conflict that lies at the heart of wet nursing among the privileged. It was considered to be the best way of nurturing the infants of the royal households, leading gradually to the favoured way of bringing up the children of those who could buy 'mother's milk' (Sussman, 1982). Yet wet nursing seemed to fly in the face of those who, from the second century AD, had the psychological insight that the wet nurse came between the natural bonding of mother and child. This conflict may begin to offer an explanation as to why wet nursing, as a method of child-rearing, has remained hidden behind the idealisation of motherhood.

Notes

1. 'An occupation . . . as old as time' (Fildes, 1988: p. 4).
2. I am indebted to Adam Elgar, who not only introduced me to Ascoli's book, but then translated several sections of it for me.
3. See Fildes, 1988: p. 2.
4. It is interesting to note that in 2014 'The United Arab Emirates has passed a law requiring mothers to breastfeed their children until they are two years old . . . [They] suggested wet nurses should be provided for children whose mothers had died or could not feed them' (*Guardian*, 8 February 2014).
5. The term 'wet nurse' was first used in English in 1620 according to the *Shorter Oxford English Dictionary* to denote someone who suckled another's child, although earlier records often refer to her as 'milk mother'. The idea of hiring another to feed one's child may have been introduced from the slave-owning societies of Greece and Rome but the term 'wet nurse' seems to have come into use in contrast to the term 'dry nurse'; she was one who did not suckle the child but looked after it and, as Dickens (1861) phrased it, brought the baby up 'by hand'.
6. 'Notable cultures which continue to employ wet nursing today are those of the Islamic faith. These still abide by the teaching of the *Koran* . . . If a wet nurse is employed, her child must still be the same sex as the child to be nursed. This is not only because the milk intended for a child of the opposite sex is believed to cause disease or death in the nursling, but more importantly, because incest might occur when the foster-siblings become adults' (Fildes, 1988: p. 269).
7. In Constantinople, in the Green Social Complex, built in 1421, there are nine sarcophagi of the family of Celebi Sultan Mehmed, including himself. The first large green tomb in the room is of the family wet nurse [information sent to the author by Dr Felicity de Zulueta].
8. Marie de Longuet de la Gaudiere was married to Jean Longuet, Seigneur Gaudiere. She was one of eight wet nurses that fed Louis XIV. Six of the other wet nurses are unnamed (fr.wikimini.org/wiki/Louis XIVdeFrance).
9. In Charlotte Zeepvat's (2006) book, *From Cradle to Crown: British Nannies and Governesses at the World's Royal Courts,* the wet nurses who fed all these royal babies, alongside their nannies, remain unnamed.
10. The continuation of this superstition was brought to my attention by Melanie Hart in an article on 'corrective rape'. A lesbian mother had her child taken away from her by her mother, who believed if she touched it or fed it 'she would make him gay' (*Independent Magazine*, 18 February 2014).
11. For similar views, see deMause (1976); Ross (1976); Sussman (1982).
12. I wish to thank Aigli Broukou for this observation.
13. The *lactaria* denoted a certain column in market cities where wet nurses could be hired or infants in need of a wet nurse would be brought (Fildes, 1988).
14. See also Badinter (2011); Sussman (1982).
15. This view is confirmed in Badinter (2011); Fildes (1988); Sussman (1982).

16. Freud suggested that Leonardo was ignorant of the physiology of the female body, 'since dissection of bodies was regarded as desecration', but Freud also believed that an early drawing that Leonardo made of the sexual act between a man and woman depicted a single duct from the woman's nipple that 'was connected in someway with the sex organs' because of the 'quite special strength' of Leonardo's 'sexual repression' (Freud, 1910c: pp. 70–3).
17. Similar views are to be found in Fildes (1988); Heywood (2001); Kertzer (2000); and Stone (1990).
18. A personal anecdote told to the author.
19. It was not uncommon for babies to have to adjust to several wet nurses during the first two or three years of life. The wet nurse might become pregnant, not produce enough milk, or she might die. Ross (1976) said that 'Adjustment to not one but to several successive *balie* was apparently the fate of many infants, and it continued to be a fatal weakness of the system' (p. 192).

References

Aeschylus (1928) *The Oresteia*, Murray (trans.). London: George Allen & Unwin.

Aristotle (1910) *The Works of Aristotle, Vol. 4: Historia Animalium*, J.A. Smith and W.D. Ross (eds). Oxford: Oxford University Press.

Ascoli, G. (1994) *Balie*. Palermo: Sellerio.

Badinter, E. (2011) *The Conflict: How Modern Motherhood Undermines the Status of Women*, Arianna Hunter (trans.). New York: Metropolitan Books; Henry Holt & Co.

Bakewell, S. (2011) *How to Live: A Life of Montaigne in One Question and Twenty Attempts to Answer*. London: Vintage Books.

Bernard, J.F. (1973) *Talleyrand: A Biography*. London: The History Book Club.

Boswell, J. (1988) *The Kindness of Strangers: The Abandonment of Children in Western Europe from Later Antiquity to the Renaissance*. London: Penguin.

Brown, S. (ed.) (1999) *Women's Writing in Stuart England*. London: Sutton Publishing.

Burdin, L.S. (2011) *Images of Woman and Child from the Bronze Age: Reconsidering Fertility, Maternity and Gender in the Ancient World*. New York: Cambridge University Press.

Castor, H. (2010) *She Wolves*. London: Faber & Faber.

Damrosch, L. (2007) *Jean-Jacques Rousseau: Restless Genius*. Boston; New York: Houghton Mifflin Company.

deMause, L. (1976) The evolution of childhood. In: *The History of Childhood*, L. deMause (ed.). London: Souvenir Press.

Dickens, C. (1848) *Dombey and Son*. London: Thomas Nelson.

Dickens, C. (1861) *Great Expectations*. London: Thomas Nelson.

Fildes, V. (1986) *Breasts, Bottles and Babies*. Edinburgh: Edinburgh University Press.

Fildes, V. (1988) *Wet Nursing. A History from Antiquity to the Present*. Oxford: Basil Blackwell.

Fletcher, A. (2008) *Growing Up in England: The Experience of Childhood, 1600–1914*. New Haven; London: Yale University Press.

Foreman, A. (1998) *Georgiana Duchess of Devonshire*. London: HarperCollins.

Freud, S. (1910c) *Leonardo da Vinci and a Memory of His Childhood*. S.E.11. London: Hogarth Press.

Gaythorne-Hardy, J. (1993) *The Rise and Fall of the British Nanny.* London: Weidenfeld & Nicolson.

Gellius, A. (2012) *The Attic Nights of Aulus Gellius*, Vol. 2, Rev. W. Belloe (trans.). Forgotten Books. www.forgottenbooks.org.

Gerhardt, S. (2004) *Why Love Matters: How Affection Shapes a Baby's Brain.* London: Routledge.

Hardin, H.T. (1985) On the vicissitudes of early primary surrogate mothering. *Journal of American Psychoanalytic Association* 33: 609–29.

Heywood, C. (2001) *A History of Childhood.* Cambridge: Polity Press.

Holmes, R. (2009) *The Age of Wonder: How the Romantic Generations Discovered the Beauty of Science.* London: Harper Press.

Homer (1946) *The Odyssey*, E.V. Rieu (trans.). London: Penguin Classics.

Hufton, O.H. (1995) *The Prospect before Her: A Woman in Western Europe, 1500–1800.* New York: Alfred Knopf.

Hyde, M. (1977) *The Thrales of Streatham Park.* London; Cambridge, M.A.: Harvard University Press.

Kertzer, D.I. (2000) The lives of foundlings in nineteenth century Italy. In: *Abandoned Children,* C. Panter-Brick and M.C. Smith (eds). Cambridge: Cambridge University Press.

Klapisch-Zuber, C. (1987) *Women, Family and Ritual in Renaissance Italy.* Chicago; London: Chicago University Press.

Leigh, D. (1616) [1999] The Mother's Blessing. In: *Women's Writing in Stuart England: The Mother's Legacies of Dorothy Leigh, Elizabeth Joscelin, and Elizabeth Richardson,* S. Brown (ed.). Thrupp, Stroud: Sutton Publishing.

Longford, E. (1964) *Victoria R.I.* London: Weidenfeld & Nicolson.

Marvick, E.W. (1976) Nature versus nurture: patterns and trends in seventeenth century French child-rearing. In: *The History of Childhood,* L. deMause (ed.). London: Souvenir Press.

Mate, M.E. (1996) *Women in Medieval English Society.* Cambridge: Cambridge University Press.

McHenry, L.C. and MacKeith, R. (1966) Samuel Johnson's childhood illnesses and the King's evil. *Medical History* 10: 386–99.

McLaughlin, M. (1976) Survivors and surrogates: children and parents from the ninth to the thirteenth century. In: *Centuries of Childhood,* L. deMause (ed.). London: Souvenir Press.

Moore, G. (1894) [1999] *Esther Waters.* Oxford: Oxford World Classics.

Nokes, D. (2009) *Samuel Johnson: A Life.* London: Faber & Faber.

Pinchbeck, I. and Hewitt, M. (1969) *Children in English Society*, Vols 1 & 2. London: Routledge & Kegan Paul.

Plutarch (2008) *In Consolation to His Wife*, Robin Waterfield (trans.). London: Penguin Books.

Pugh, G. (2007) *London's Forgotten Children: Thomas Coram and The Foundling Hospital.* Stroud: Tempus Publishing.

Ross, J.B. (1976) The middle-class child in urban Italy, fourteenth to early sixteenth century. In: *The History of Childhood,* L. deMause (ed.). London: Souvenir Press.

Shorter, E. (1977) *The Making of the Modern Family.* New York: Basic Books.

Shorter Oxford English Dictionary (1973) Oxford: Oxford University Press.

Soranus of Ephesus (1956) *Soranus' Gynecology*, O. Temkin *et al.* (trans.). Baltimore: Johns Hopkins.

Stone, L. (1990) *The Family, Sex and Marriage in England 1500–1800* (abridged). London: Penguin Books.

Sussman, G.D. (1982) *Selling Mother's Milk: The Wet-Nursing Business in France, 1715–1914.* Urbana; Chicago; London: University of Illinois Press.

Zeepvat, C. (2006) *From Cradle to Crown: British Nannies and Governesses at the World's Royal Courts.* Gloucester: Sutton Publishing.

Chapter 2

The foundling and the wet nurse

In 1496 on the border of the Allier river in the Haute-Loire in France, a little girl of six, Marguerite Romeuf, found a stone which she hit against another stone and when it cracked open there was revealed within a small Madonna and Child, no more than 15 millimetres in height and painted in gold and azure. This treasure has become known as 'The Madonna of the Foundling', or 'Notre-Dame Trouvée'. Every year there is a pilgrimage in early July when the Madonna, now safely held in a reliquary, is paraded around the village of Lavoute-Chirac where she was found.

This legend, and much hangs upon how 'Notre-Dame Trouvée' is translated, is believed by some to be the Madonna of the Foundling, that is to say 'Trouvée' becomes 'Les Enfants Trouvées' or 'abandoned infants'. For others the 'Trouvée' refers to the fact that she was found by an infant. However, if 'Notre-Dame Trouvée' is taken as the iconic figure of the unwanted child, this helps to keep the image in mind and it serves as a reminder that there has been a tendency to forget about the extent of infant abandonment throughout history (Boswell, 1988).[1]

The last chapter was concerned with highlighting some of the reasons for wet-nursing among those who could afford to buy 'mother's milk'. But an equally significant part that wet nursing has played throughout recorded history is in nurturing the 'succourless poor child' (Pinchbeck and Hewitt, 1969: p. 126).

This is where Boswell's (1988) exhaustive research, *The Kindness of Strangers*, on infant abandonment, is important in the light of what it reveals about the part the wet nurse played in keeping alive those babies who had been abandoned or orphaned. Without her ample breasts many unwanted babies found on dung heaps, mountainsides and in rivers would have had no chance of survival. Through her ministrations such figures as Moses, who it is true was in the end fed by his mother, when she posed before the Pharoah's daughter as a wet nurse, Mohammed and, we could conjecture, Oedipus, have lived to become iconic figures in cultural, mythical and religious history.

Fildes (1988) suggested that the abandonment of infants was relatively rare in the Ancient Near East; however this was not the case in early Greek and Roman civilisations. 'Children were abandoned throughout Europe from Hellenistic Antiquity to the end of the Middle Ages in great numbers, by parents of every social standing, in a great variety of circumstances' (Boswell, 1988: p. 428). Boswell gives a number of reasons for the abandonment of children, and is keen to point out that most abandoned children were rescued and thus their mortality rate was not much higher than infant mortality more generally. Boswell also emphasises that infant abandonment was never a moral or ethical issue, and was therefore never condemned. The reasons for infant abandonment were most often social, that is to say, parents were starving or ill or there was a war or plague or they had too many children (Fildes, 1990). Illegitimacy was another important reason for abandoning an infant, especially if the mother was unmarried. Many young servants were seduced by their employer and had to get rid of the child if they were to continue in employment (McLaughlin, 1976). The wish to avoid conflicts over inheritance among the better off could also lead parents to dispose of a second or third son, for it was not until the thirteenth century that the rule of primogeniture became Roman law and then the disposal of a second son could be avoided (Boswell, 1988).

Boswell (1988) claimed that although 'the historical writing on abandonment in late antiquity and The Middle Ages has been meager' (p. 39) the most extensive period of infant abandonment occurred during the Roman Empire. It was seen as a method of controlling the size of the family, for contraceptives were not known. One result was that the number of abandoned infants probably stood between 20 and 40 per cent (Kertzer, 2000). The unwanted child might be sold in the market place, during this period, or hung upon a tree or put on a dung heap. Later, with the coming of Christianity, the infant might be placed on the doorsteps of a church, or, when a little older, he or she might be placed in a monastery.[2]

Boswell argues that one of the reasons that no moral indictment was attached to the abandonment of children was that it was differentiated from infanticide, which was universally condemned.[3] He poetically describes how Romans might have felt when they abandoned their children.

> Society relied on the kindness of strangers to protect its extra children, a kindness much admired and prominent in the public consciousness. Even a wild animal could be expected to feel tenderness toward exposed children: Romans looked up to see, in the center of their city, the statue of a wolf who had suckled two abandoned children and in so doing helped to found their empire.
>
> (Boswell, 1988: p. 433)

The Romans could take comfort from the belief that their abandoned children would be rescued for, as Boswell pointed out, there was a subtle distinction between infanticide and abandonment. In the case of abandonment there was a hope that hanging your child from a tree or putting it in a public place would arouse someone's wish to rescue it; in this way infant abandonment was seen as a good method of controlling family size. Aristotle endorsed such an idea with an image from the natural history of the eagle. The eagle would lay three eggs, hatch two and throw out one (Kertzer, 2000: p. 84). Therefore it was quite natural to throw out a child or two. What seems to be missing in such an image is that the eagle within the egg that is thrown out necessarily dies and so such an analogy in fact condones infanticide. A more chilling example is given by Socrates in the *Theaetetus*, in which he says that a new idea should be compared with a newborn infant – 'is it worth bringing up? . . . do you imagine that any child of yours should necessarily be reared and not abandoned?' (Kertzer, 2000: p. 83). It has been argued, of course, that Socrates is merely using the newborn infant as a metaphor, therefore Boswell is probably right to conclude that it was morally acceptable to abandon unwanted children in early Greek and Roman society, even if a sleight of hand was needed in order to assert that it was not to be considered as infanticide.

What is common to all the accounts of infant abandonment, whether the reasons were economic, social or psychological, is that abandonment was seen as a way of avoiding the crime of infanticide; Laius could safely sleep in his bed for he had not killed his child, Oedipus, he had merely abandoned him. Furthermore, as Boswell suggests, the abandonment of children was sustained by a belief that not only would the child be found but it might have a better life. Perhaps Freud's suggestion that many children create a 'family romance' (1909c) in which they imagine they come from royal descent has its historical origins in the 'family romance' that underpinned many societies who abandoned their children. The parents believed that their abandoned children were going on to a better life, and in some cases this must have been true.

Throughout the history of infant abandonment, there have been those who dissented from the popular idea that the abandoning of infants was culturally or morally acceptable (McLaughlin, 1976). A dramatic way of bringing to the attention of parents one consequence of their actions was voiced by an early Christian, Clement of Alexandria (150–216 AD), who put it this way, 'How many fathers, forgetting the children they have abandoned, unknowingly have sexual relations with a son who has become a prostitute or a daughter become a harlot?' (Boswell, 1988: p. 3). Was the fate of Oedipus not a similar warning to Greeks who abandoned their children?

The outcome for the abandoned infant shifted significantly with the spread of Christianity in Europe in the seventh century. Unwanted babies could now be placed in the porches of churches, which may have been a little safer, though there still remained the problem of how they should be looked after. This led to the Church setting up foundling hospitals across Europe, of which the first was built in Milan in the eighth century.[4] These hospitals would take in unwanted babies where they would be fed by wet nurses. There were experiments in 'dry-nursing' or feeding them 'by hand' but this method of feeding usually led to the infant's death. Paradoxically it seems that infant mortality in fact increased once abandoned babies were shut behind the doors of foundling hospitals, even though it was imagined that this was to be a more humane way of treating unwanted children. Not only were foundling hospitals breeding grounds of infection but the wet nurses who were employed to feed these babies tended to be of the poorest class

(Fildes, 1988). They were often on the edge of starvation themselves and desperate for any work, and as can be imagined, they would not have an overflowing amount of milk for these babies. Nevertheless they would be expected to take on three or four babies at a time and yet receive an insufficient wage. In fact they would be paid less than any other category of wet nurse. 'The allowance of these women being scanty, they are tempted to take part of the bread and milk intended for the poor infants. The child cries for *food,* and the nurse beats it *because* it cries' wrote Hanway (1712–1786) (Fildes, 1988: pp. 283–4). One consequence was that the most undernourished wet nurses with the least milk were succouring the most deprived infants in the community. And this situation was true whether in Russia (Dunn, 1976) or France (Sussman, 1982) or England (Fildes, 1988). It is therefore not surprising to discover that the condemnation of the wet nurse has centred on her care of the motherless baby.

It was not until the eighteenth century that figures for the number of abandoned children in England and across Europe were kept more systematically (Kertzer, 2000). These newly collected figures make clear that the number of abandoned infants was staggeringly high, though it needs to be remembered that in this century there was a population explosion across Europe with the rise of industrialisation and the growth of towns. In France, the French Revolution led to extreme poverty and a substantial increase in abandoned infants (Fildes, 1988) with the result that in Toulouse, 'one child in every four was *known* to have been abandoned' (Boswell, 1988: p. 15). Not surprisingly many foundling hospitals, whether in France or other parts of Europe, were hard pushed to find enough wet nurses for the burgeoning number of infants who were left at their doors. To take one of the worst figures, in the years 1750–1759 in Dublin the mortality rate for these unwanted children was 89 per cent; in England between 1741 and 1759 the figures were slightly better and about 50 per cent died (Fildes, 1988: p.156).[5]

Boswell (1988) suggested that when we look at some of these appalling mortality figures we also need to remember that it was not just the care that the abandoned infant received in the foundling hospitals that led to their early death, but many arrived drugged and starving and would have had little chance of survival anyway. The poor state of health of some of these infants is confirmed in a report on the first intake of infants into Coram's Foundling Hospital in 1745. They were described in the following way: 'Many of them appeared as if Stupified with Opiate, and some of them almost starved, or as in the agones of Death thro' want of Food, too weak to Suck, or to receive Nourishment' (Pugh, 2007: p. 14).

It is extremely painful to read about the suffering of these millions of unwanted babies throughout the ages and so it is with a certain relief to turn to Coram's Foundling Hospital, for it stands as a beacon of concern for those illegitimate infants who had been abandoned or for children whose mothers no longer had the wherewithal to look after them. Coram stands not only as a beacon of concern, but in following the history of the setting up of the Foundling Hospital and the subsequent treatment of these unwanted babies, his concern also illustrates a social and cultural shift that was taking place in the eighteenth century about the care of unwanted children. Thomas Coram struggled for 17 years to raise the money and get permission from George II to build the first and only foundling hospital in England. He succeeded in 1739. There was much opposition to such an idea for it was thought that it would encourage the profligate poor to be even more feckless. But Coram felt impelled to redress the appalling suffering he witnessed as he walked the streets of London. Many infants lay abandoned on heaps of rubbish. There is no doubt that Coram was moved by the suffering he saw on the streets of London, though some have suggested that the social willingness to support his endeavour was not entirely philanthropic but a more realistic appreciation that the population needed to increase in order that the many wars being waged at the time could have a ready supply of 'cannon fodder'. Greater concern was given to extending the life of children, for they were seen as a 'natural resource' for military services (Pugh, 2007: p. 31).

Coram's Foundling Hospital opened its doors in 1745 and the first 30 children were taken in. Twenty-three of them died within the first few months so Coram realised that if these infants were to be given some chance of survival they needed to be moved out of the hospital as quickly as possible (Pugh, 2007: p. 35). He resorted to a practice that had long been in use by the middle classes, namely 'farming out' his foundlings to wet nurses in the country, and the mortality rates decreased rapidly; not least because the wet nurses that these infants went to were more prosperous and better nourished than the impoverished wet nurses in the city. These Coram foundlings fared better than any other foundlings in Europe; for instance in France, between 1773 and 1777 80 per cent of all foundlings died, whereas in London, between 1741 and 1759 only 56 per cent died (Fildes, 1988: p. 156).

The foundlings from the Coram Hospital might live for five to seven years in their foster family, and from many more recent accounts that have been given by foundlings, they looked back on these years as idyllic (Adie, 2005; Pugh, 2007). 'Mrs Palmer was a lovely cook and it was an absolutely idyllic life for a young child' (Pugh, 2007: p. 120). Fildes (1988) did extensive research into a group of wet nurses in Hertfordshire who fed the Coram infants and she found these children had had a good life and, from most accounts, were lovingly looked after by a considerate wet nurse. There was a nice irony, as Boswell pointed out, about Coram's decision to 'farm out' foundlings to wet nurses in the country. This was exactly what the rich and privileged had been doing for centuries and so for these foundlings there was a moment of democracy or equality between the rich and the poor; they were all receiving the same sort of nurturing experience for several years.

A memorable bond was often created between the wet nurse and her foundling and so it is not surprising to discover that both suffered when the time came to part. In 1765, the Rector of Northchurch in Hertfordshire wrote to the London Foundling Hospital that Elizabeth Nash and her husband wished 'to take back the children they had left there about a fortnight since' (Fildes, 1988: p. 186). In other words, the foundlings they had brought up for many years had become much-loved members of their family. However they were not allowed to take back these children, for they were 'of an age to be taught a trade' (Fildes, 1988: p. 187). The heartbreak for them all is painful to imagine, though perhaps there is some comfort in the thought that some of these 'farmed out' foundlings must have had a brief period with warm-hearted foster mothers. These women were often bringing up their own children, and far from bureaucratic rules, they might become pregnant or continue to breast feed their own baby alongside the foundling (Fildes, 1988: pp. 174–89). So it is safe to assume that some of the Coram foundlings would have had a few years of family life.

The shock came when the foundlings were returned to the Foundling Hospital. A heartbreaking account is given by Hannah Brown, who described her return in the following way, 'I . . . sank into the nonentity which the child who enters a Pauper Institution is bound to become' (Pugh, 2007: p. 98). There are other written accounts by Coram's foundlings who were left bewildered and deeply ashamed of their situation. They wrote about the gradual erosion of their personality through the institutional rules that disciplined them at every moment of the day. This loss of personality was accompanied by feelings of shame about their origins, and guilt that it was their fault that they were now imprisoned in a place that was cut off from all contact with the outside world – 'all the time at the back of your mind, you were thinking, "What's happened to me? Where did I come from? . . . what have I done?" And begin to feel guilty that you've done something to cause it' (Pugh, 2007: p. 129). For others the Foundling Hospital experience eroded their trust in relationships and they experienced difficulty in creating their own family. As one foundling said, 'I think the biggest effect is probably family, because you don't know how to live with a family: you don't know how to live with a wife and you don't know how to bring up children' (Pugh, 2007: p. 135). Perhaps one of the best summaries of the foundling experience is the one written in the nineteenth century by the same Hannah Brown, quoted above, who wrote, 'these "unwanted children" without a mother, friend or relative in the world. . . . are forced to submit to all the injustices and degradations which arise when they are thrown into the hands of complete strangers' (Pugh, 2007: p. 99).

All the children returned to the Coram Foundling Hospital were set to learn a trade and found their lives one of harsh discipline along military lines. As one of the governors was to write, these foundlings were never to forget that they must 'learn to undergo with Contentment the most Servile and laborious Offices; for notwithstanding the innocence of the Children, yet as they are exposed and abandoned by their Parents, they ought to submit to the lowest stations' (Pugh, 2007: p. 40). At an early age, somewhere between 11 and 16, the boys would be apprenticed and leave the Foundling Hospital. Boswell chillingly describes the more general European fate of those who left their foundling hospitals. They were 'classless, familyless, unconnected adolescences with no claim on the support or help of any persons or groups in the community' (p. 421). On Pugh's (2007) account the Coram Foundling Hospital did continue to be interested in the boys until they had fulfilled their time of indenture at 21. For girls it was slightly better as they could stay in the hospital and work, and they might even be given a small dowry when they married (Fildes, 1988; Kertzer, 2000).

We saw in the last chapter that the practice of handing over one's child to a wet nurse aroused many fears among the rich and privileged. There were always voices that were critical of the nurse, especially in the cases where the child failed to thrive. However when it comes to the wet nurse of the 'succourless poor child', in the foundling hospitals and other care homes and workhouses across Europe, she receives an altogether more lurid portrait: 'traditional *nourrices* seem to have had virtually no intrinsic interest in the welfare of infants. If one died, they would simply go back to the hospital and be given another. . . . Children were commodities for them' (Shorter, 1977: pp. 185–6). They were described as 'slovenly' and 'dirty' (Stone, 1990: p. 27) or 'Angel makers' (Panter-Brick, 2000: p. 1), working in a system that was no more than 'an organized system of infanticide' (Fildes, 1988: p. 210). An eighteenth-century midwife in England, Elisabeth Nihell, writing in 1760 about the unwanted child said, 'not one poor babe of the thousands taken in have escaped general destruction . . . except one boy, of whom it is recorded as a prodigy, that he lived till he was five years of age' (Fildes, 1986: p. 282).

It is therefore no surprise to discover that at the start of Coram's Foundling Hospital there was a prejudice against employing wet nurses. The governors of the hospital tried to persuade Coram that it would be much better to bring up these children 'by hand' within the institution. But it is clear that their argument was underpinned by economic considerations as well as an emotional distaste for the wet nurse. The governors believed that not only was the luxury of 'mother's milk' too good for the foundlings but they also argued that bringing them up 'by hand' was less of a burden upon the state. One of the governors, Robert Dingley, added a nice psychological twist against wet nursing; he asked, how could a wet nurse be 'so unnatural as to give the least share of milk to her own child whose natural right it is?' (Fildes, 1988: p. 168). What Dingley was struggling to accommodate goes to the heart of the discussion about abandoned babies; what was the cheapest way to bring them up? Many of those who were in a position to rule on how to save the lives of unwanted infants shared Dingley's distaste for wet nurses; yet at the same time it was becoming evident that infant mortality was very high if they were fed 'by hand'. The hand of the governors, as it were, was being manipulated by the statistics; foundlings fed by wet nurses in the country survived much better than those brought up in institutions. But what emerges out of this debate about the slovenly wet nurse is the beginning of a new attitude towards her and the rights of the infant of the wet nurse.[6] Ironically Dingley's argument did in the end help to consolidate the more general arguments against wet nursing.

As already suggested, Coram's Foundling Hospital was a beacon of light in the darkness that surrounded the care of unwanted babies. A hundred years later, in England, foundlings were still dying in their thousands and one of the chief reasons for the high mortality figures was that parishes were unwilling to give more than a grudging amount of money to keep alive these unwanted children and would scarcely pay the wet nurses a living wage. Little was done to save the lives of these foundlings until a notorious scandal about 'baby farming' rocked London in 1849 and the last vestiges of the eighteenth-century method of 'farming the poor' (Pinchbeck and Hewitt, 1969: p. 508) in England came slowly to an end. A Mr Drouet ran a 'privately operated' home for foundlings in Tooting. He took in about 1400 orphans from several parishes in London, and it was believed they were benefiting from the country air that surrounded Tooting at the time. Cholera broke out in this home and 180 children died. A health inspector visited this 'baby farm' and he discovered starving and unhappy children living in 'inexcusable neglect'. Charles Dickens was to write four excoriating articles on Drouet's establishment in *The Examiner* following his trial.[7] The cholera epidemic was attributed to the poor diet and the overcrowded conditions under which the children were living. Drouet was brought to court, and even though there was a damning report on the condition under which the children lived, he was found not guilty on the grounds that it could not be proved that the children would not have died anyway (www.workhouses.org.uk/drouet). If the Drouet scandal helped to bring to an end the 'baby farming of the poor' in large institutions, the belief that the wet nurses of these abandoned babies were no better than 'angel makers' still echoed in the minds of those concerned about how to nourish the 'succourless poor'. And they continued to be described as 'indigent, filthy and decrepit' women who beat the starving infants if they cried (Pinchbeck and Hewitt, 1969: p. 178).

This prejudice against the notorious 'angel maker' was brought forcibly to the public mind in 1870. If, as Pinchbeck and Hewitt (1969) suggested, the last vestiges of the eighteenth-century method of 'farming the poor' (p. 508) had been brought to an end with the Drouet scandal in 1849, the problem still remained of what to do with unwanted babies. In 1870, 276 bodies of children under one week old were found in Brixton and Peckham. This, unsurprisingly, aroused popular concern and a Sergeant Relf was sent to investigate. He tracked down a 'Mrs Oliver' who advertised in a local newspaper that she was willing to adopt any unwanted child and give it a loving home. She charged a premium of £5. Sergeant Relf managed to find the house where she lived and called. There he discovered 10 young babies asleep and drugged with laudanum. Five of them subsequently died and 'Mrs Oliver' and her assistant were charged with murder and found guilty; 'Mrs Oliver' was executed and her assistant was imprisoned. One of the points that was made against her at her trial was that she knew that bringing up a child 'by hand' 'would probably accomplish or accentuate its death' (Pinchbeck and Hewitt, 1969: pp. 613–15). There followed on from this scandal and the previous one at Tooting, the Infant Life Protection Act of 1870, and 'baby farming' became outlawed. It is not clear whether the particular babies that 'Mrs Oliver' was looking after were handed over to her by women who were seeking work as a wet nurse; but there is enough evidence to show that many young women who had just given birth to an illegitimate child and needed to sell their milk to survive, would have resorted to farming their baby out to a 'Mrs Oliver', as in the case in George Moore's (1894) literary account of Esther Waters (see Chapter 4).

The problem of 'baby farming' was not unique to England. In France in 1866 Dr Charles Monot wrote a report on the 'baby farming' of the babies of wet nurses. He produced statistical evidence to show that these babies from a region in Burgundy died because they were 'farmed out' and brought up 'by hand' while their mothers found good employment as wet nurses in Paris, or Lyon or Marseille. These Burgundian wet nurses would live with the family who employed them and the conditions of their life were much improved. They usually earned enough money to send some back to their family, and their diet and the living conditions were considerably better than those they had left behind, but when they returned home their own babies most often would be dead (Sussman, 1982).

Before the eighteenth century there had been scant consideration for the child of the wet nurse.[8] Soranus thought the ideal wet nurse should have had a son of two months old before she offered her milk to another child. He believed that her milk would then be at its best. But what did he imagine happened to her two-month-old son? On this he was silent. And it is interesting to discover that the manuals and rules that were written about how to find the best wet nurse all fail to mention how the child of the wet nurse should be looked after. One of the first documents that considers the fate of the wet nurse's baby is to be found in the Bureaux of Wet Nursing in Paris. Here in its Laws and Ordinances in 1762 a statement was drawn up that recommended that 'The "age" of a nurse's milk must not be less than seven months old, to protect the nurse's own baby' (Fildes, 1988: p. 125). This was the beginning of a new realization that the babies of wet nurses were dying of neglect and starvation from lack of 'mother's milk' (p. 196). However, in spite of this increased awareness about the 'natural rights' of the wet nurse's child, whether in France or in other parts of Europe, the babies of the wet nurse continued to die when they were separated from their mother. And this 'sentence of death' (Sussman, 1982) became an increasingly pressing concern by the nineteenth century.

These scandals and the more rigorous collection of mortality rates helped to bring about a noticeable shift in concern for the abandoned infant of the wet nurse by the late eighteenth century. In 1871 further questions were being asked in *The British Medical Journal* as to whether 'a mother should be asked to sacrifice her child'. It was observed that 'a much larger destruction of infant life results from the wet-nursing system' because it entailed the wet nurse 'putting out' her own child (Fildes, 1988: pp. 196–7). There were other concerns that had been voiced from time to time which helped to turn the tide against wet nursing, or more accurately, there was an acknowledgement of the risk that wet nurses took on when they agreed to feed abandoned babies. From the fifteenth century onwards there was a recognition that wet nurses could catch syphilis from these infants. In many cases the foundlings were the illegitimate children of prostitutes who had picked up the disease from merchants and sailors who were travelling the world. The disease would be passed to the infant, who in turn could transmit it to the wet nurse. If the wet nurse contracted the disease she might pass it on to her husband and all the rest of her family. If that was the case she could expect to be compensated if she did become ill, but this was an added expense to the state and no payment could alleviate the destruction that she and her family would unwittingly suffer.

As we have seen, Boswell (1988) had suggested that abandoning unwanted infants had been part of European culture since Roman times, and furthermore, he had argued, no shame was attached to this way of dealing with a surfeit of children. Paradoxically, once the Church and other charitable organisations began to assume the responsibility for unwanted children there was an unintended consequence. It became accepted that any unwanted baby could be placed in the foundling hospital and it was believed that it would be well looked after. While this provision was an essential means of lessening human suffering for those without the means to care for their child, it nevertheless helped to support an attitude towards unwanted children that can seem quite heartless today. For instance, Rousseau (1712–1778), a well-educated man, saw fit to take his five children to a foundling hospital in Paris, as though it was the obvious thing to do in the circumstances. It was only much later that he lived to regret his actions, but at the time of giving up his children he wrote, 'This arrangement seemed so good and sensible and right to me' and so,

> My third child therefore was taken to the Foundling Hospital like the others, and the next two were disposed of in the same way, for I had five in all . . . if I did not boast of it publicly it was solely out of regard for their mother . . . I really saw no wrong in it . . . All things considered, I made the best choice for my children, or what I thought was the best for my children.
>
> (Rousseau, 1765: pp. 333–4)

Similarly, in 1778 Lorenzo Da Ponte, Mozart's famous librettist, placed his two illegitimate children in the Pieta Foundling Hospital in Venice. He was a Roman Catholic priest so his children would have been an inconvenient encumbrance to his profession, but this did not lead him to express a sense of shame about his conduct. And furthermore in his *Memorie* (1823) there is no mention of his children, unlike Rousseau, and so we can assume he truly believed that this was the best way of dealing with his unwanted children (Bolt, 2007).

It is surprising to discover that in the twentieth century there was still a similar belief that there need be no shame attached to abandoning an infant. It was believed that the state could provide 'delegated motherhood' (Hrdy, 1992: p. 409) for abandoned children, and furthermore that this 'delegated motherhood' was 'a logical extension of child fostering, passing on responsibility for a child to the state rather than to kin or neighbours' (Panter-Brick, 2000: p. 15). What such an argument seems to ignore is the feelings of both those who are abandoned and the mothers who are, for whatever reason, forced to give up their children. While it is undoubtedly true that many foundling hospitals did do magnificent work in trying to keep alive these unwanted children, nevertheless to describe foundling hospitals as providing 'delegated motherhood' is to gloss over the suffering that accompanies infant abandonment. In the Coram Hospital today there are exhibited painful notes that mothers pinned to their child when it was left at the door. Some were given names; others had pinned to their clothes distressing accounts of how the mother had been abandoned by their father and could no longer find enough food for them; there were other fervent notes that expressed hope they might one day take back their child. It is clear from these notes that mothers felt both pain and shame at having to delegate their mothering to an institution; and for most of their children this delegated mothering could not possibly compare with how it might have been if they had been fostered or given to a neighbour.

In reflecting upon the history of infant abandonment, it is hard not to believe that their suffering has been 'a nightmare from which we have only recently begun to awaken' (deMause, 1976: p. 1). But it has been a nightmare shared by all. The foundling felt guilty to have been the cause of abandonment, ashamed that he or she was probably illegitimate and despairing to be without a home in the world. The wet nurse was often burdened by poverty and yet she was expected to feed more babies than she could manage; she was also expected to carry the many abusive comments about her capacity to keep these babies alive. Her own child would often meet a hasty end when it was sent to a 'baby farm' where it was fed 'by hand'. At the same time, there were many impoverished mothers who were heartbroken at having to hand their infant over to be cared for by the state because they were destitute.

Just as the wet nurse of the rich and privileged is scarcely mentioned by social historians of the family, it is equally true that in this painful history of the unwanted child, the wet nurse seldom enters the pages of social history. She has two pages in Aries' (1962) *Centuries of Childhood*; even in Stone's (1990) extensive research into *The Family, Sex and Marriage in England, 1500–1800* she is almost non-existent and in one of the most recent books, Cunningham's (2006) *The Invention of Childhood*, she does not appear at all. Why has there been a tendency to airbrush the wet nurse, whether of the rich or the poor, out of our social history? Has there been a general cultural taboo in thinking about her? As already mentioned, Fildes (1986), as an historian, had asked why feminist social historians had ignored this important job. Whichever way we look at the wet nurse she inhabits an ambiguous place in the hearts of those she has fed and in the minds of those who have employed her. She has been much needed but she has also been much despised. The following chapters will continue to pursue the question as to why there has been a silence surrounding the wet nurse of both the rich and the poor.

Notes

1. It would be wrong to imagine infant abandonment has died out. 'Earlier this year, the Beijing Youth Daily said the hospital that treats abandoned babies found in the capital had received more than 10,000 in the past decade' (*Guardian*, 29 May 2013). Or in 'The Southern Chinese city of Guangzhou' they have 'suspended a "baby hatch" programme that allowed patents to abandon infants safely and anonymously, because a local welfare centre could not cope with the number of arrivals' (*Guardian*, 18 March 2014).

2. This last procedure was known as 'oblation' deriving from the Latin *oblatio* meaning 'offering', and was a particularly cruel form of abandonment. This was no longer infant abandonment, because the child might be about seven years of age, but once it had been handed over to the monks, it had no freedom whatsoever for the rest of its life. It was worse than slavery. The child could never leave the monastery or marry or have any social or political rights, though for the abandoning parents they could be assured that at least the child would be fed and looked after (Boswell, 1988: p. 228; McLaughlin, 1976).
3. In 374 AD infanticide became a capital offence in Roman Law (Lyman, 1974).
4. In 787 AD, Datheus, Archbishop of Milan was moved to found an asylum for illegitimate children who would be looked after until the age of eight (Lyman, 1974; McLaughlin, 1976).
5. There is, however, one delightful account of the use of goats in a foundling hospital in Aix in France in 1775. Their foundlings were dying from lack of wet nurses, and so direct suckling by goats was tried, and this was the account: 'the cribs are arranged in a large room in two ranks. Each goat which comes to feed enters bleeting [sic] and goes to hunt the infant which has been given to it, pushes back the covering with its horns and straddles the crib to give suck to the infant. Since that time they have reared very large numbers in that hospital' (quoted in Fildes 1988: p. 146). Perhaps the use of the wet nurse in foundling hospitals would have ended more rapidly if this strange story had been more widely known!
6. Hannah Moore (1745–1833) when she heard of Mary Wollstonecrafts' *Vindication of the Rights of Women* (1792) remarked, 'We will be hearing of the Rights of Children next' (quoted in Brendon, 2005: p. 35).
7. Dickens' four articles in *The Examiner* in 1849 on the condition of these pauper children in Drouet's orphanage emphasised that 'if the system of farming pauper children cannot exist without the danger of another Tooting Farm being weeded by the grisly hands of Want, Disease, and Death, let it now be abolished' (27 January 1849) (www.workhouses.org.uk/drouet).
8. In 1875 Charles E. Buckingham wrote that because the child of the wet nurse would usually lie in an unmarked grave, its mother could have had no feeling for it: 'the death of her own child, which frequently happens as a consequence, disturbs her but very little' (Fildes, 1986: p. 200).

References

Adie, K. (2005) *Nobody's Child*. London: Hodder & Stoughton.

Aries, P. (1962) *Centuries of Childhood: A Social History of Family Life*, R. Baldick (trans.). New York: Alfred A. Knopf.

Bolt, R. (2007) *Lorenzo Da Ponte: The Extraordinary Adventures of the Man behind Mozart*. London: Bloomsbury.

Boswell, J. (1988) *The Kindness of Strangers: The Abandonment of Children in Western Europe from Later Antiquity to the Renaissance*. London: Penguin.

Brendon, V. (2005) *Children of the Raj*. London: Phoenix, Orion Books.

Cunningham, H. (2006) *The Invention of Childhood*. London: BBC Books.

deMause, L. (1976) The evolution of childhood. In: *The History of Childhood*, L. deMause (ed.). London: Souvenir Press.

Dickens, C. (1849) *The Examiner*. www.workhouses.org.uk/drouet.

Dunn, P.D. (1976) 'That enemy is the baby': childhood in imperial Russia. In: *The History of Childhood*, L. deMause (ed.). London: Souvenir Press.

Fildes, V. (1986) *Breasts, Bottles and Babies*. Edinburgh: Edinburgh University Press.

Fildes, V. (1988) *Wet Nursing: A History from Antiquity to the Present.* Oxford: Basil Blackwell.

Fildes, V. (1990) Maternal feelings re-assessed: child abandonment and neglect in London and Westminster, 1550–1800. In: *Women as Mothers in Pre-Industrial England*, V. Fildes (ed.). London; New York: Routledge.

Freud, S. (1909c) *Family Romances.* S.E.9. London: Hogarth Press.

Hrdy, S.B. (1992) Fitness tradeoffs in the history and evolution of delegated mothering with special reference to wet-nursing, abandonment, and infanticide. *Ethology and Sociobiology* 13: 409–42.

Kertzer, D.I. (2000) The lives of foundlings in nineteenth century Italy. In: *Abandoned Children*, C. Panter-Brick and M.C. Smith (eds). Cambridge: Cambridge University Press.

Lyman, R.B. (1974) Barbarism and religion: late Roman and early medieval childhood. In: *Centuries of Childhood*, L. deMause (ed.). London: Souvenir Press.

McLaughlin, M. (1976) Survivors and surrogates: children and parents from the ninth to the thirteenth century. In: *Centuries of Childhood*, L. deMause (ed.). London: Souvenir Press.

Moore, G. (1894) [1999] *Esther Waters.* Oxford: Oxford World Classics.

Panter-Brick, C. (2000) Nobody's children? A reconsideration of child abandonment. In: *Abandoned Children*, C. Panter-Brick and M.T. Smith (eds). Cambridge: Cambridge University Press.

Pinchbeck, I. and Hewitt, M. (1969) *Children in English Society*, Vols 1 & 2. London: Routledge & Kegan Paul.

Pugh G. (2007) *London's Forgotten Children: Thomas Coram and The Foundling Hospital.* Stroud: Tempus Publishing.

Rousseau, J.-J. (1765) [1954] *The Confessions*, J. Cohen (trans.). London: Penguin Books.

Shorter, E. (1977) *The Making of the Modern Family.* New York: Basic Books.

Soranus of Ephesus (1956) *Soranus' Gynecology*, O. Temkin *et al.* (trans.). Baltimore: Johns Hopkins.

Stone, L. (1990) *The Family, Sex and Marriage in England 1500–1800* (abridged). London: Penguin Books.

Sussman, G.D. (1982) *Selling Mother's Milk: The Wet-Nursing Business in France, 1715–1914.* Urbana; Chicago; London: University of Illinois Press.

Chapter 3

The second mother

The wet nurse was believed to be a necessity in royal households throughout the world; she became a status symbol in many families of the rich and she was an essential life-saver to the orphaned or abandoned child. One noteworthy feature of wet nursing is that there was a substantial body of evidence, from Aulus Gellius in the second century AD, Rousseau in the eighteenth century, to deMause in the middle of the twentieth century, suggesting that the wet nurse came between the natural bonding of mother and child, yet this was seldom taken into account. This fact is further reflected in most social history, biography and psychology, where little interest has been shown in the possibility that a wet nurse might take the place of the mother in the psyche of the child. It is as though there has been a collective unconscious wish to turn a blind eye to the idea that the wet nurse might become a 'second mother' or an internal model for a 'first wife'. Yet Robert Louis Stevenson celebrated his nurse in just this way.[1] Such an idea strikes at the heart of the cultural values given to the mother and the family in Western Europe and as a result it has been socially inconceivable that the nurse might become the centre of the child's emotional life. In spite of this cultural reluctance to imagine the role the wet nurse might play in the psychic formation of the child she nurses, her 'impression' can be discerned in some biographies of those who are known to have had a wet nurse.

It could be said that the Western cultural ideal of motherhood, which continues to this day, reached its peak in the early Renaissance. The paintings of the Madonna and Child often depict a tender encounter with Mary and the Christ Child unswaddled, unlike most babies at that time (Fildes, 1988). In others she seems preoccupied with concerns about his future, for the Christian message of man's suffering and redemption is of course the primary demand of these works. But if we step back into the social landscape that surrounded these paintings and ask where their psychological power comes from, there is a startling contrast between these iconic paintings of Mary and her Child and the actual life that many of the artists who depicted her will have experienced in their infancy.

In northern Italy between 1300 and 1550, most middle-class infants were sent away from home into the arms of a wet nurse, or *balia* (Klapisch-Zuber, 1985; Ross, 1976). Leonardo was taken away from his mother at an early age and was then brought up by his stepmother (Freud, 1910c). Michelangelo was sent into the country to a wet nurse (Nardini, 2009). These facts raise an interesting question as to whether an aspect of the portraits of the Madonna and Child were representing a cultural aspiration or a longing for maternal tenderness as well as expressing a spiritual message about man's suffering. Has the wish for maternal adoration always been more in the mind than reality? Klapisch-Zuber (1985) in her book *Women, Family and Ritual in Renaissance Italy* suggested that the sacred imagery of this early art reflected not only 'hypermaternal attitudes that the devotional texts attribute to the Virgin herself' but also 'permitted young women, shut up from childhood in a convent, or subjected to a distant husband and separated from their own children at birth to identify with the mother of Christ and transmute their frustrations and tensions' (p. 326). In a similar vein, Ross (1976) wrote,

> Actually a child at this age, about a year or so, was probably lying swaddled and immobile, and often miserable and underfed, at the mercy of a wet-nurse miles away from its mother. In the pictures, [of the Florentine Renaissance] the child reigns supreme over the mother, the sole object of her love and attention.
>
> (p. 199)

Whatever one believes about the truth of the observations raised by Klapisch-Zuber and Ross, at the very least, 'farming out' middle-class children into the homes of the wet nurse created a split between the idealisation of motherhood and the reality of maternal care.

There has been an ongoing debate about the role of the wet nurse and whether she confirms the view that the 'history of childhood is a nightmare from which we have only recently begun to awaken' (deMause, 1976: p. 10).[2] But there is another debate that runs through the history of childhood and is concerned with whether maternal care and love has changed even if the methods of child-care are different (Heywood, 2001).[3] In a nutshell, do women love and care for their children more today than they did in the past? In looking at the history of wet nursing, the use of a wet nurse does not necessarily mean maternal dereliction or lack of maternal love and concern; in the words of Mary Verney, in Chapter 1, sending one's child into the country with a wet nurse could be a heartbreaking affair for the mother. But whether you are fed at your mother's breast or at the breast of a wet nurse, there is a difference that is both physical and psychological.

There are few autobiographical accounts that even record the existence of a wet nurse; this is partly because those who write about their early life will have little memory of her presence, unless she has been in their lives when conscious memory begins at the age of about three (Schore, 2002). But it is also the case that the significance of being fed at the breast of someone other than one's mother has seldom been thought to be of interest whether one turns to historians, biographers or psychoanalysts.

It is therefore necessary to stretch the imagination when exploring the possible 'impression' of the wet nurse upon the well-recorded lives of Michelangelo, Rousseau, Talleyrand, Austen and Nabokov. Michelangelo (1475–1564), in Vasari's (1511–1574) account, 'jokingly declared: "Georgio. If I have any intelligence at all, it has come from being born in the pure air of your native Arezzo, and also because I took the hammer and chisels with which I carve my figures from my wet-nurse's milk"' (Vasari, 1550 [1991]). The fantasy is delightful, but how to understand the psychological significance of his fantasy is more problematic. Are we to believe that Michelangelo had identified with his wet nurse and her husband, who was a stonecutter? Vasari writes that Michelangelo's father had inherited land around Arezzo, where there were many quarries, and so it is possible that the husband of Michelangelo's wet nurse was employed by Michelangelo's father. Would this have made a difference? Michelangelo was certainly 'farmed out' to his wet nurse in Settignano (Nardini, 2009) but it is not recorded how long he stayed in her family. His belief that he had become a stonecutter through the influence of the husband of his wet nurse poses another question as to whether Michelangelo's life and even character were influenced not only by the milk of his wet nurse but by her relationship with her husband. An even more challenging question is whether Michelangelo's actual parents might have been less central to Michelangelo's sense of himself or of his identity than the family of this wet nurse. His mother died when he was about six, and a recent biographer (Nardini 2009), suggested that his father thought 'art was disgraceful. He saw no difference between a painter and a whitewasher, between a stonemason and a sculptor' (p. 11). Even if we cannot be sure whether Michelangelo did identify himself with his wet nurse and her husband, his supposed jocular statement to Vasari does give rise to a socially uncomfortable idea that a child could be influenced by its wet nurse, even if she and her family are of a lower class and economically dependent.

The idea that an infant at the breast of a wet nurse may have positively identified with her raises many interesting psychological questions. It is much more disturbing to imagine that the emotional life of an infant may have been distorted by a negative experience at the breast of a wet nurse. Rousseau (1712–1778) put his five children into a foundling hospital in Paris (see Chapter 2), but his behaviour becomes more comprehensible when his early life is known. Jean-Jacques Rousseau's mother died in childbirth and he was raised by his unmarried aunt Suzanne and a 16-year-old nursemaid Jacqueline (Damrosch, 2007). There is no mention of a wet nurse in Damrosch's account, however in 1712 Rousseau would probably not have survived if he had been brought up 'by hand', that is to say, fed on 'bread and water pap or other unsuitable cereal foods and gruel' (Fildes, 1988: p. 97), and therefore the supposition is that there must have been a wet nurse as well as Suzanne and Jacqueline.

The 'impression' of his caretakers echoes throughout Rousseau's life and work; that is to say, Rousseau is haunted by the loss of his dead mother and her replacement by several unsatisfactory substitutes. Rousseau describes with great tenderness the songs Suzanne sang to him. He also wrote about Jacqueline that she had been 'his sole consoler' when he was locked in a garret for several days. However he seems to have regretted their care, for about Suzanne he wrote, 'I forgive you for having kept me alive' and about Jacqueline 'if my good Jacqueline had not taken such pains to preserve me when I was little, I would not have suffered such great misfortunes after I grew up' (Damrosch, 2007: pp. 12–13). Here he seems to be expressing a melancholy bitterness that reaches back to the loss of his mother and his wish that he had died with her.

In early adulthood Rousseau embarked upon an idealised love affair with Mme de Warens, an older woman who had separated from her husband. Rousseau conceived a romantic image of her and came to call her 'Mamma'. He said the relationship was not 'a love relationship, but a more real possession, dependent not on the senses, on sex, age or personal beauty, but on everything by which one is oneself, and which one cannot lose except by ceasing to be' (Rousseau, 1781: p. 213). In the same vein he goes on to say, 'I became entirely her concern, entirely her child, and more so than if she had been my mother' (pp. 212–13). However, this relationship changed dramatically when Mme de Warens took him to her bed. Then Rousseau was filled with unaccountable feelings: 'I tasted the pleasure, but I knew not what invincible sadness poisoned its charm. I felt as if I had committed incest and, two or three times, as I clasped her rapturously in my arms I wet her bosom with my tears' (pp. 189–90).

There were several other unsatisfactory encounters with idealised women that continued throughout most of his life, but in his mid-30s Rousseau settled into a relationship, that was to last until his death, with Therese Lavasseur. She was an uneducated woman who could scarcely read or write and it was only towards the end of his life that Rousseau married her. The role Therese assumed was of nurse and housekeeper; they lived in separate rooms and Therese appeared only in order to serve meals to Rousseau and his friends and she seldom accompanied him on social occasions, yet he was deeply dependent upon her to look after him (Damrosch, 2007).

The role that Therese assumed in Rousseau's life had, however, a traumatic consequence. They had five children and Rousseau with the help of Therese's mother put each of their children on the day of their birth into a foundling hospital. Why? In his *Confessions* (1781) he said he did not have the means to support them. While that was undoubtedly true, a more psychological explanation would suggest that he was repeating or acting upon his own experience of being orphaned. If this psychological explanation is correct, he must have, nevertheless, hoped that they would be fed by a wet nurse, for that was the only hope of survival in a foundling hospital in eighteenth-century France. It is this idea that lends support to the hypothesis that Rousseau himself had had a wet nurse, who had kept him alive, even if he wished he had died.

No traces of his children have been found, so we do not know what happened to them. But when Rousseau became an internationally revered educationalist he tried to find his eldest daughter, because one of his female friends had offered to adopt her, but he discovered he had not given her a name and so no record could be found (Damrosch, 2007).

Twenty years after his first child was born Rousseau wrote his famous polemic on child education, *Emile* (1762). It was a revolutionary book that had an important influence, not so much on education as on the current child-rearing practices of eighteenth-century Europe, where sending swaddled babies out to wet nurses was the favoured way of bringing up middle-class children (Rousseau, 1762). Rousseau held a philosophical belief that man was naturally good but that this natural goodness is distorted by society, and so his argument against wet nurses and swaddling reflect his view that they are both unnatural and have a deforming social effect upon the child. His argument that it is unnatural for mothers to send their children away to a wet nurse reveals an interesting psychological observation. He begins by saying, 'The woman who nurses another's child in place of her own is a bad mother; how can she be a good nurse?' And then he goes on and adds, 'She [the wet nurse] may become one in time; use will overcome nature, but the child may perish a hundred times before his nurse has developed a mother's affection for him.' However, if the child does experience a 'mother's affection' from his wet nurse, then a profound conflict takes place within the psyche of the child. When the child is returned to its biological mother, she will realise that the child loves its wet nurse and not her. As a consequence the mother will teach the child 'to look down on their nurses, to treat them as mere servants'. But now comes the sting in the tail – this will prepare the child 'to despise at a later day the mother who bore him, as he now despises his nurse' (Rousseau, 1762: p. 14).

There is such a passionate ring to what he writes in this early part of *Emile* that it is hard not to believe he is speaking from his own experience. The question is how to interpret what he is saying. His argument against wet nurses confirms the view that he was fed by a wet nurse, but we need to see his anger with wet nurses in *Emile* also in relationship to the abandonment of his five children. It makes sense to assume that this behaviour is linked to his own unhappy experience in early childhood, a motherless childhood with a wet nurse and two other caretakers, but what needs to be added is that the wet nurse has a highly ambivalent place in his feeling and imagination. She saved him, yet it is a life he wishes not to have had. It is this same ambivalence that is visited upon his children. Their lives are to be saved but they are confined to having a 'bad mother'/wet nurse. Throughout his life he could not resolve the paradox of a 'bad mother'/wet nurse who sustained life but who could never become a 'good nurse/good mother'. In its stead he struggled with an internal image of his own dead mother who forbade him to love those who nursed him, or in the case of his own children, those who needed him.

How was he able to persuade Therese to voluntarily give up her own children? It could be said that when Rousseau met Therese he had unconsciously chosen someone who fulfilled some of his needs. She was on all account his 'servant', but tragically she was not able to help him find a way through his traumatic start in life, or to put it more harshly, she was not able to stand up to him with maternal authority when she bore his children. Instead, by agreeing to abandon her own children, she colluded with him in repeating his trauma (Coles, 2011). But that was not the end of the matter for he came to be haunted by his behaviour and in *Emile* he wrote,

> Who ever cannot fulfill the duties of a father has no right to become one. Neither poverty nor labors nor other people's judgment can exempt him from nourishing his children and bringing them up himself. Readers, you can believe me. I predict that anyone who has a heart and neglects such sacred duties will weep long and bitterly for his error, and will never be consoled.
>
> (Rousseau, 1762: pp. 262–3)

Returning to Rousseau's experience of feeling that he had committed incest when he made love to Mme de Warens, here is another example of his lifelong conflict between goodness and society, or put another way, between reason and passion. Why did he feel he had committed incest? In the above account, Rousseau's difficult life seems to have been complicated by a search, in adulthood, for a lost maternal relationship. His caretakers had never been able to help him through his loss, or offer a substitute model of maternal care that he need not despise. His persistent search for a maternal object was necessarily complicated by sexual desire when he reached adulthood. His infantile sexual desire and his adult capacity for full sexual intercourse did not 'marry up'. His initial desire for Mme de Warens was to be her child, not a sexual object, but this desire wobbled at a boundary that was not clearly demarcated, for of course she was not his mother. In the intimacy of a shared life he came to feel adult sexual passion for her and wished 'to possess this beloved object'. This wish to possess her was no longer an infantile wish for he felt 'the inability to control my desires and my imagination to a sufficient extent to remain master of myself' (Rousseau, 1781: p. 188). But nevertheless there was a clash between his adult desire and his stronger infantile wish for a maternal object with the result that their consummation felt like incest.

A sexual conflict in adulthood that Rousseau experienced runs through many accounts of the lives of those whose mothers either died in childbirth or who were farmed out to wet nurses. It is as though the incest barrier that naturally grows up between a mother and child is not so firmly fixed in the cases where the woman who suckles is not the mother of the child. One reason may be that the wet nurse seldom stays with the child into adulthood, and therefore she can become an imaginary figure in the internal world, either despised for her abandonment or searched for in the streets of desire. Rousseau suffered inconsolably from repeating his childhood trauma upon his own children, but also what seems clear from reading Rousseau's *Confessions* is that in all his relationships with women, whether with Mme de Warens or Therese, someone was missing, not only his mother but also a permanent helpful and nurturing internal figure. He was either hopelessly under the spell of an imaginary Mother/Madonna, as with Mme de Warens, or, as in the case of Therese, in a relationship with a woman whose maternal feelings he could effectively obliterate, or, perhaps more accurately, despise.

The truth of Rousseau's (1762) observation that it is unnatural to send a child to a wet nurse and then expect the child to love its mother when it is returned, is confirmed by the experience of Jane Austen (1775–1817), who never recovered a warm relationship with her mother after she was sent out to be wet nursed for the first year or 18 months of her life (Tomlin, 1997). This was a pattern of infant care that Jane Austen's other siblings had experienced, and in many ways it was much less traumatic than the fate suffered by those who were 'farmed out' at a greater distance and who did not see their parents for several years. Austen's mother visited her daily, yet in spite of this contact Austen had with her mother, the experience of being wet nursed created a distance between mother and child that never healed. And maybe one can hear Austen's indignation at her treatment when, in *Emma* (1816), she has Isabella Knightley express outrage at the idea of a parent sending a young child away from home:

> There is something so shocking in a child's being taken away from his parents and natural home! I can never comprehend how Mr. Weston could part with him [Frank Churchill]. To give up one's child! I really never could think well of anybody who proposed such a thing to anyone else.
>
> (p. 87)

The experience of Talleyrand (1754–1838), who was 'farmed out' to a wet nurse, is an even more traumatic example of the dislocation that can take place between the child and its parents. Talleyrand, at his birth, was sent to a wet nurse in the suburbs of Paris, and there he lived for the first four years of his life and was never visited by his parents (Bernard, 1973). He described these early years of his life in his memoirs as 'spent cheerlessly' (Bernard, 1973: p. 20). When he was four and still living in the home of his wet nurse, he remembered, 'I accidently fell from the top of a chest and dislocated my foot' (p. 19). Some months later his parents were informed and they were concerned enough to try and get his foot properly set, but it was too late, and for the rest of his life, Talleyrand had to wear a special shoe and an iron brace on his leg, and he walked with a crutch. But even at that moment in his life, Talleyrand's parents did not take him back into the family; instead he was sent off to the country for two years to live with his great grandmother. Here, for this brief time, he experienced being loved; an important experience that was repeated throughout his adult life in his many love affairs. But this experience was brought to an abrupt end when his parents sent him off to boarding school. This sudden separation from his great grandmother left him feeling, 'isolated, helpless, shut up in myself' (Bernard, 1973: p. 25). More bitterly he was later to write, 'I am perhaps the only member of a large and distinguished family who never, in his entire life, had the good fortune to spend one single night under the same roof as his parents' (p. 28).

He learned to temper his emotional distress with the reflection, 'these first disappointments of my life taught me to bear misfortune and disappointment with indifference, and to meet such things with the resources which my self-knowledge taught me I possessed' (p. 29). And while it is true that he became the greatest statesman of his time, exercising the diplomatic skills of stubborn insistence with a political philosophy that was based on the principle of law, he lived most of his emotional life as a libertine, probably fathering three children. Women who met him fell under his spell, not only his intellectual brilliance but also his sexual magnetism. On Bernard's account these passionate relationships did not last but he maintained friendships with his mistresses throughout his life. He did eventually marry but only for political expediency at the insistence of Napoleon. He always felt the marriage was against his will. It was therefore not surprising that the marriage came apart when Napoleon fell from power. Talleyrand then formed a relationship that continued throughout the last 20 years of his life, with his niece by marriage, the Duchess de Dino, who was 40 years younger than him. The story of their relationship is complex and has interesting incestuous echoes to Rousseau's relationship with Mme de Warens.

Before Talleyrand formed this relationship with his niece, the Duchess de Dino, he had arranged her marriage to his nephew, Edmond. Talleyrand was by this time middle aged and it had become clear to him that he would never have any legitimate children to inherit his money, his land and his titles. He decided to make his nephew Edmond his heir, but Edmond was not married and did not look as though he would be able to find a suitable wife. So Talleyrand looked around and chose the young and beautiful Duchess de Dino to be Edmond's bride. The Duchess de Dino had an equally beautiful and widowed mother, the Duchess de Courland. During the marriage arrangements Talleyrand fell passionately in love with the Duchess de Courland and they had a relationship that was much valued by both of them. Unsurprisingly the marriage that Talleyrand had arranged between his nephew Edmond and the Duchess de Dino was an unhappy one and they soon separated. At this point Talleyrand left the Duchess de Courland and formed a relationship with her daughter, the Duchess de Dino.

The nature of their relationship has been much speculated upon. What is known is that they lived in the same house in Paris and the Duchess de Dino gave birth to a daughter, Pauline. There is no definite evidence that this child was Talleyrand's daughter, though the whole of Paris believed she was. Certainly Talleyrand adored the child, and treated her with the love and consideration that he had not given to his other two illegitimate children and he left her property and wealth when he died. Even if we can never know whether Talleyrand had a sexual relationship with his niece the Duchess de Dino or whether he was the father of Pauline, Talleyrand and the Duchess de Dino seem to have had a relationship that broke many boundaries. She was the wife of his nephew and her mother had been his mistress; furthermore when he was still married he took the Duchess de Dino rather than his wife to Vienna when he was negotiating the important Congress of Vienna (1814–1815).

Are there echoes of being 'farmed out' to a wet nurse and away from his family that Talleyrand repeated in the complicated relationships he had with women and not least with the Duchess de Dino? Unlike Rousseau there is not such a clear split between idealised women and denigrated maternal figures; Talleyrand's 'indifference' is more calculated. He wanted women who were brilliant and attractive but who would help him gain the positions of power he needed in public life. Most of his mistresses were able to fulfil this function and the Duchess de Dino helped him supremely well throughout his later political career, for she was young, beautiful and highly intelligent. Their salon, whether in Vienna, Paris or London, was the one that everybody wished to attend and much political finessing took place during these sought-after social occasions (Bernard, 1973).

It could of course be said that many children suffer from the absence of parental love and that Talleyrand's experience was not exceptional. Zeigler (1962) writing about the great French families of the eighteenth and nineteenth centuries remarked that 'there was little room for children and only in the most exceptional cases did parents play a significant part in the education and upbringing of their children' (p. 178). Although this may have been a socially acceptable pattern that many parents followed, all children need love and attention, whatever the cultural and moral values of the time. The fate that awaited a child who had neither the loving care of a mother nor of a wet nurse was always uncertain. Rousseau and Talleyrand stand as witnesses to the psychological dislocation that can follow the absence of a constant loving presence in the early years of life. At the very least they could not be fathers to their own children. Talleyrand had to find a way of managing the 'indifference' of his wet nurse and his 'indifferent' parents. In the case of Rousseau, though he seems to have been loved and cared for by his aunt Suzanne and the 16-year-old Jacqueline, he never recovered from his complicated feelings about his mother's death and the loss of a wet nurse.

A more contemporary figure who had a wet nurse was Vladimir Nabokov (1899–1977). Can her 'impression' be imagined in his writing? Nabokov was, on his own account, an adored eldest son. In fact he was a second son. Nabokov's mother had given birth to a still-born son the year before Nabokov's birth (Boyd, 1990). This was an event that was not considered significant in accounts of the author's life. It is not difficult, however, to hear that this dead brother is obliquely present in the opening paragraph of Nabokov's autobiography, *Speak, Memory* (1969) in which the first line reads, 'The cradle rocks above the abyss'. This haunting image is followed by Nabokov's reflection that 'Our existence is but a brief crack of light between two eternities of darkness'. These two opening sentences of his autobiography give rise to the question as to why he felt like that. The next sentence provides an interesting answer. He remembers his panic when he had been shown an early homemade movie, which had been made a few weeks before he was born. In the first image his mother was waving from a top floor window 'as if it were some mysterious farewell'. This was followed by a second image, in which 'what particularly frightened him [and notice he puts himself as the object of this reflection] was the sight of a brand-new baby carriage standing on the porch, with the smug, encroaching air of a coffin' (Nabokov, 1969: p. 17). It would not be stretching the imagination too far to suggest that the panic which Nabokov experienced on seeing the home movie was about his own mortality, projected onto him by his mother, who feared she might be waving farewell to him, her second son, as she had to her eldest son. If we put together these three ideas, 'The cradle rocks above the abyss', 'Our existence is but a brief crack of light between two eternities of darkness' and the image of the 'brand-new baby carriage' that might turn into a 'coffin', it seems clear that an emotional darkness had accompanied Nabokov's birth. He had no words to describe his own fear that he was following in the footsteps of a brother who had died at birth but he could feel his mother's dread that he might not survive.

Following Nabokov's birth, he was handed over to a wet nurse, in the tradition of most Russian nobility (Dunn, 1976). When the wet nurse finished suckling him, he was looked after by what he called 'a bewildering sequence of English nurses and governesses' (Nabokov, 1969). 'This bewildering sequence' of people who looked after him became entwined in his imagination with a sexually complex family history that he later embellished in his writing. His great grandmother, Nina, a noteworthy beauty at the Russian Court of Alexander II, had an illicit affair with Dimitri Nabokov. In order to more safely pursue her affair, she married off Dimitri to her 17-year-old daughter (Field, 1988). The interest in noting Nabokov's family history is that he uses it to provide a structure for his subtle exploration of emotional longings that hinge upon the forbidden. In two novels, *The Enchanter*, written in 1939 but published posthumously in 1986, and *Lolita*, published in 1955, he inverts his own family ancestry so that the two central characters marry mothers in order to appease their lust for the two daughters.[4]

In both novels there is a large age gap between the two heroes, Arthur and Humbert Humbert, and the nymphets they are pursuing. This is striking and one way of thinking about the meaning of this age gap is to see it as a reflection of 'a psychic pain' that 'puts time out of joint' (Hoffman, 2011: p. 95).[5] In other words, a fundamental time structure was 'out of joint' in the psyches of both Arthur and Humbert Humbert, and this led them in a search for a timeless figure, who tragically remained enigmatic, shadily sexual and just out of emotional reach.

Nabokov wrote *The Enchanter* in Russian and it lay unpublished and forgotten until his son translated it and published it in 1986 after Nabokov's death. However in the appendix that Nabokov wrote to *Lolita* in 1956 he commented that 'the first little throb' that had inspired him to write *The Enchanter* had 'never quite ceased' and 'began to plague me again'. And so, as he said, he felt inspired to rewrite *The Enchanter* but in English, 'the language of my first governess . . . the nymphet with a dash of Irish Blood' (Nabokov, ed. Appel, 1991: p. 312).

Nabokov dismisses the idea that he had any purpose when he wrote *Lolita*, though he does say that he was going to destroy the manuscript when he had finished the book, but he was stopped 'by the thought that the ghost of the destroyed book would haunt my files for the rest of my life'. He also says that *Lolita* had been a 'comforting presence' and adds that 'this glow . . . in an ever accessible remoteness is a most companionable feeling' (Nabokov, ed. Appel, 1991: p. 315).

Nabokov on all accounts was a writer who chose his words with great precision (Boyd, 1990; Nabokov, 1986), so it is surely significant that he chose the word 'throb' twice to describe the way he was plagued by the idea of *Lolita*. What does he intend by that word? The *Oxford Shorter English Dictionary* defines throb as 'to beat strongly esp. as the result of emotion or excitement'. Nabokov's first emotion/throb had led him to write *The Enchanter,* in Russian, but 'the throb' had not been quietened; he continued to be plagued and he had to start again, as it were. What seems to have been significant was that he wrote this same tale in English, 'the language of my first governess . . . the nymphet with a dash of Irish blood' (Nabokov, ed. Appel, 1991: p. 312).

If we put together Nabokov's first 'throb' of excitement, which led him to write *The Enchanter,* and his second 'throb', which compelled him to rewrite the novel in English, the language he associated with his English governess, a complicated pattern begins to emerge. The opening sentence of *The Enchanter* has Arthur say 'How can I come to terms with myself?' (Nabokov, 1986: p. 21). Is this what is exercising Nabokov throughout his creative career? Is he the type of artist, as Beckett once said about Proust, who has 'an inner text that they need to translate'? (Bracewell, 2012). Was Nabokov's inner text about how to come to terms with 'throbs' of excitement that can be aroused at surprising and unaccountable moments?

What is significant is that in both novels, *The Enchanter* and *Lolita*, there is the theme of a grown man longing for a child to provide a 'comforting presence'. Yet having written these two novels, he put aside *The Enchanter* and thought he had lost it and he actually took the manuscript of *Lolita* to the incinerator, where his wife Vera rescued it. Was Nabokov wishing to disavow their distressing and inverted subtexts? Both novels could be seen as creative descriptions of the 'abyss' Nabokov had encountered at his birth, following the death of his brother, compounded by other losses, such as the loss of his mother's breast, the loss of his wet nurse, 'a bewildering sequence of English nurses and governesses', and finally his loss of fortune and country following the Russian Revolution. However when Nabokov describes the way that *The Enchanter* was inspired by a 'first little throb' that had 'never quite ceased' and how this then led him to rewrite it in English as *Lolita,* we are in a world that is freighted with connotations of adult sexual excitement. What gets lost, in translation as it were, is that both Arthur and then Humbert Humbert are searching for lost and enigmatic figures from childhood bound up with 'throbs' of infantile passions, but these infantile passions are compromised by the confusion with adult sexual appetite. This leaves them, as Humbert Humbert says in *Lolita*, in a world split between 'two sexes, neither of which were mine' (Nabokov, 1986: p. 18).

For Rousseau and Talleyrand, their adult sexual relationships were tinged with infantile incestuous fantasies. These incestuous fantasies occur as a way of trying to make sense of or come to terms with loss. If the enigmatic presence of a caretaker/wet nurse disappears suddenly, there is not enough time to consolidate her as a comforting internal presence. She leaves the infant with fantasies that cannot be resolved. The infant is left imprisoned in a timeless warp that ignites infantile sexual desire. This is a way of bringing comfort to the self as the infant tries to come to terms with the disappearance of the caretaker. In the case of Nabokov he felt his early years were golden and full of love. While there is no reason to doubt his words, what has aroused so much difficulty in Nabokov's writings is the pain we can hear, especially in these two novels. Arthur's longing for his 'nameless nymphet' and Humbert Humbert's desire for Lolita are metaphoric expressions of an infantile longing for a comforting or enduring presence. What Nabokov has helped us understand is the legacy of the multiple and indefinite shadows of a dead brother, an anxious mother, a lost wet nurse and a 'bewildering sequence of English nurses and governesses', peering into the cradle above the abyss and terrifying the child with their fleeting presences. And as if to confirm such an idea, Nabokov (1964), in *The Real Life of Sebastian Knight*, wrote, "Remember that what you are told is really threefold: shaped by the teller, reshaped by the listener, concealed from both by the dead man of the tale' (p. 44).

In tracing the complicated lives of Michelangelo, Rousseau, Austen, Talleyrand and Nabokov, one can see that their experiences in early childhood at the breast of someone who was not their mother may have had a profound effect upon their emotional and sexual lives. The absence of interest in the wet nurse, in many biographical and autobiographical accounts of those who have had one, gives rise to the thought that she has been difficult to accommodate into the history of the family, with its cultural and social emphasis on the importance of the biological parents. In some cases, such as that of Michelangelo, he seems to have cherished the memory of his wet nurse and her 'mother's milk', but few parents would want to imagine that the wet nurse and her family had such an important influence upon their child. If we turn to Rousseau or Talleyrand a more difficult picture emerges of the wet nurse. She may have been a deforming influence, to use the metaphor of Talleyrand's damaged foot; or she may have provided little love or attention, as with Rousseau; or broken the bond between mother and child, as with Austen. In the case of Nabokov, the death of his brother, the loss of his mother's breast, followed by the losses of his wet nurse, and his 'bewildering sequences of English nurses and governesses' can be heard echoing, tantalisingly, throughout the pages of *The Enchanter* and *Lolita*. In all these lives the wet nurse, whether remembered or not, casts a melancholy shadow upon the psyche of the child she has fed.

Notes

1. R.L. Stevenson (1905). *A Child's Garden of Verses.*

   'For the long nights you lay awake
   And watched for my unworthy sake:
   For your most comfortable hand
   That led me through the uneven land:
   For all the story books you read:
   For all you pitied, all you bore,
   In sad and happy days of yore:-
   My second Mother, my first Wife,
   The angel of my infant life –'

Stevenson (1850–1889) was an only child who had a weak chest, with severe breathing problems. It may have been tuberculosis, and he certainly suffered ill health all his life, dying at the early age of 44. This poem records his tender affection for the nurse who looked after him through his early life. In his 30s he married a woman who was 10 years older than him, and who had already been married with three children. She also looked after him devotedly. See Woodhead (2001).

2. For a similar point of view see Aries (1962); Shorter (1977); Stone (1976).
3. See also Pollock (1987); Vickery (1999).
4. Field (1988) writes that the love affair between Nina and Dimitri was 'one of the great secrets of the Nabokov family'. He goes on to say that this incestuous secret becomes a familiar theme in Nabokov's fiction. In Nabokov's final novel, *Solus Rex,* written in Russian, he has a psychiatrist say that 'psychic problems derive not from one's parents but from the problems of one's ancestors' (p. 7).
5. 'Trauma has no past, no present, no future, but persists in a non-time that can be presented continuously, making the event ever present' (Mucci, 2013: ps. 43–4).

References

Aries, P. (1962) *Centuries of Childhood: A Social History of Family Life*, R. Baldick (trans.). New York: Alfred A. Knopf.

Austen, J. (1816) *Emma.* London: Nelson Classics.

Bernard, J.F. (1973) *Talleyrand: A Biography.* London: The History Book Club.

Boyd, B. (1990) *Vladimir Nabokov: The Russian Years.* London: Chatto & Windus.

Bracewell, M. (2012) "You are selling people things inside themselves that they've forgotten they have." Damian Hirst at Tate Modern. *Tate Magazine* 25: 42–50.

Coles, P. (2011) *The Uninvited Guest from the Unremembered Past.* London: Karnac.

Damrosch, L. (2007) *Jean-Jacques Rousseau: Restless Genius.* Boston; New York: Houghton Mifflin Company.

deMause, L. (1976) The evolution of childhood. In: *The History of Childhood,* L. deMause (ed.). London: Souvenir Press.

Dunn, P.D. (1976) "That enemy is the baby": childhood in imperial Russia. In: *The History of Childhood,* L. deMause (ed.). London: Souvenir Press.

Field, A. (1988) *VN: The Life and Art of Vladimir Nabokov.* London: Futura Press.

Fildes, V. (1988) *Wet Nursing: A History from Antiquity to the Present.* Oxford: Basil Blackwell.

Freud, S. (1910c) *Leonardo da Vinci and a Memory of his Childhood.* S.E.11. London: Hogarth Press.

Heywood, C. (2001) *A History of Childhood.* Cambridge: Polity Press.

Hoffman, E. (2011) *Time.* London: Profile Books.

Klapisch-Zuber, C. (1985) *Women, Family and Ritual in Renaissance Italy.* Chicago; London: Chicago University Press.

Mucci, C. (2013) *Beyond Individual and Collective Trauma: Intergenerational Transmission, Psychoanalytic Treatment, and the Dynamics of Forgiveness.* London: Karnac.

Nabokov, V. (1964) *The Real Life of Sebastian Knight.* London: Penguin Books.

Nabokov, V. (1969) *Speak, Memory.* London: Penguin Books.

Nabokov, V. (1986) *The Enchanter.* London: Picador, Pan Books.

Nabokov, V. (1991) *The Annotated Lolita*, A. Appel (ed.). New York: Vintage Books, Random House.

Nardini, B. (2009) *Michelangelo: Biography of a Genius*, C. Frost (trans.). Firenze: Giunti.

Pollock, L. (1987) *A Lasting Relationship: Parents and Children over Three Centuries.* London: Fourth Estate.

Ross, J.B. (1976) The middle-class child in urban Italy, fourteenth to early sixteenth century. In: *The History of Childhood*, L. deMause (ed.). London: Souvenir Press.

Rousseau, J.-J. (1762) [1993] *Emile*, P.D. Jimack (ed.). London: Everyman; J.M. Dent.

Rousseau, J.-J. (1765; 1781) [1954] *The Confessions*, J. Cohen (trans.). London: Penguin Books.

Schore, A.N. (2002) Advances in neuropsychoanalysis, attachment theory, and trauma research: implications for self psychology. *Psychoanalytic Inquiry* 22: 433–84.

Shorter, E. (1977) *The Making of the Modern Family.* New York: Basic Books.

Shorter Oxford English Dictionary (1973) Oxford: Oxford University Press.

Stevenson, R.L. (1905) [2008] *A Child's Garden of Verses.* London: Puffin Books.

Stone, M.H. (1976) Middle class childhood between 1500 and 1800: examples of the lives of artists, musicians, and writers. *Journal of the American Academy of Psychoanalysis* 4(4): 545–74.

Stone, L. (1990) *The Family, Sex and Marriage in England 1500–1800* (abridged). London: Penguin Books.

Tomlin, C. (1997) *Jane Austen: A Life.* London: Viking.

Vasari, G. (1550) [1991] *The Lives of the Artists*, J.C. Bondanella and P. Bondanella (trans.). Oxford; New York: Oxford University Press.

Vickery, A. (1999) *The Gentleman's Daughter: Women's Lives in Georgian England.* New Haven; London: Yale University Press.

Woodhead, R. (2001) *The Strange Case of R.L. Stevenson.* Edinburgh: Luarth Press.

Zeigler, P. (1962) *The Duchess of Dino: Chatelaine of Europe.* London: Phoenix Press.

Chapter 4

The wet nurse in literature and biography[1]

The wet nurse can cast a melancholy shadow upon the psyche of the child she has nurtured, especially when she disappears suddenly out of the life of the child when he or she is weaned. In such cases the child finds this early attachment broken and has to adapt to a mother who is often no more than a stranger. At the same time a socially complex picture of the shadow of the wet nurse emerges in literary examples, autobiographies and biographies when considering racial and class differences. It could be said that the social, psychological and political demands that have been made upon the wet nurse have meant that she has had an 'impossible profession' (Malcolm, 1982).

One of the best political descriptions of the 'impossible profession' of the wet nurse is Dickens' (1844) imaginative portrait of Polly in his novel *Dombey and Son*.[2] A social predicament that was very common in the middle of the nineteenth century was the death of the mother in childbirth, and in Dickens' novel, this was the fate of the infant Paul. Paul's father, Dombey, was then compelled to employ a wet nurse. Dombey applied to a London Lying-In Hospital and learned that Polly had given birth to a son who was five weeks old.[3] Polly was summoned to Mr Dombey's house and she arrived with her five children, her husband and her sister. When she accepted the job of wet nurse to Paul, Dickens made the nice point that she was expected to hand over her five-week-old son and her other four children to her husband, who was to be helped by her unmarried sister. And furthermore, as was usually the case with wet nurses, Polly was not to see any of her children while employed by Dombey. Dickens, in describing Polly's sister as 'ummarried', was making the critical point that Polly's son would not be having the comfort of 'mother's milk', and if he was to survive it would be through the hazardous method of being 'dry nursed', or being brought up 'by hand' (Fildes, 1988).

Dickens imagined Polly was a good wet nurse to Paul and that she gave him devoted love and care, but, and this was crucial to the tension in the novel, Dickens believed that the strength of maternal feeling could not be obliterated. He had Polly secretly return to her family taking Paul and his older sister with her. At the same time, Dickens understood how her employer, Mr Dombey, would be aroused to a destructive and incandescent fury when he discovered his rules of employment had been broken. Polly was dismissed and Paul never recovered from this 'second deprivation' (Dickens, 1844: p. 78) and eventually died.

In this novel, Dickens seems to be have been able to inhabit imaginatively the many conflicts that can accompany wet nursing. We get an intricately woven picture of the experience of the wet nurse and her emotional meaning to Paul, as well as the struggle her employer had when he realised that he could not control her. Dickens also seemed to be making a social comment upon the way in which employers have turned a blind eye to difficulties surrounding wet nursing. This self-deception was memorably described in a speech that Dombey makes when the contract of Polly's employment is finalised.

> It is not at all in this bargain that you need become attached to my child, or that my child need become attached to you. I don't expect or desire anything of the kind. Quite the reverse. When you go away from here, you will have concluded what is a mere matter of bargain and sale, hiring and letting and will stay away. The child will cease to remember you; and you will cease, if you please, to remember the child.
>
> (Dickens, 1844: pp. 28–9)

Dickens is one of the first novelists to tackle the emotional problems associated with wet nursing and he was not afraid of showing its potentially destructive side if the wet nurse suddenly disappears. The child might die. How many parents, as they sent their children away to wet nurses, must have deceived themselves into believing that this was a mere monetary contract and the question of love and attachment need not disturb their considerations? What Dickens highlights is the nature of this self-deception; he understood that a child can die from the loss of a loving attachment. Many writers since the second millennium have been telling parents that babies become deeply attached to those who nurture them. Dickens' literary imagination brings to life the knowledge that an infant requires a constant presence during its early years if it is to flourish.

The literary description of an equally loving wet nurse is to be found in Shakespeare's *Romeo and Juliet*. Shakespeare like Dickens had the intuitive insight that employing a wet nurse brings unintended emotional consequences, not only to the child she nurses but to the nurse herself and her family. Shakespeare subtly weaves in and out of the relationship the wet nurse has with Juliet, Juliet's parents and her own child, Susan; a relationship between wet nurse and nursling that was threaded through with love, suffering and finally tragedy.

It is not made clear in the play whether Juliet is 'farmed out' to her wet nurse or only goes to the home of her wet nurse when her parents are away in Mantua. What is certain is that the Nurse, when she is first employed, is nursing her own child as well as Juliet, which would suggest that Juliet is in the Nurse's home. The Nurse's own daughter Susan soon dies for there was not enough milk for both Susan and Juliet. Shakespeare has the Nurse say about the death of her daughter Susan, 'She was too good for me' (Shakespeare, 1595 [1994]; Act 1, Scene 3). This phrase, in its quiet understatement, allows us to imagine the Nurse's suffering as she comforts herself with thoughts of the afterlife for her child. Yet in spite of her loss we never doubt that the Nurse loves Juliet; and there is a humorous moment when she reminds Juliet of her weaning when Juliet was three. The Nurse's husband put wormwood on her nipples and Juliet became 'tetchy' and fell out 'with the dug' (Act 1, Scene 3). However, unlike the more general weaning practices of the time (Fildes, 1988), Juliet still remained within the comforting orbit of her Nurse. If Juliet was fortunate that she was not suddenly taken away from her Nurse at weaning, this did not shield either of them from other darker social betrayals that followed upon this relationship.

As Juliet enters early adolescence the Nurse aids her in her secret marriage to Romeo. This is a marriage that Juliet desires and the Nurse supports and furthers. However this marriage was unacceptable to Juliet's parents because of the political conflict between the families of Romeo and Juliet, the Montagues and the Capulets. The marriage desired by Juliet's parents, that she should marry Count Paris, and Juliet's secret marriage to Romeo, endorsed by her Nurse, bring to the fore the different social values of Juliet's parents and those of the Nurse. The inner representation of Juliet's earliest and loving relationship with her Nurse is in contrast to the distant relationship and values of her parents. That is to say, Juliet's emotional desires to marry the man she loves follows on from the loving relationship she has had with her Nurse, whereas her parents' wish is that she should be an object whom they can use to further their political ambitions (Pinchbeck and Hewitt, 1969).

'Hang thee younge baggage, disobedient wretch / I tell thee what, get thee to the church a' Thursday / Or never after look me in the face. / Speak not, reply not, do not answer me' (Act 3, Scene 5). These are the words Juliet's father uses to address her and they are a chilling reminder of his political values and his social power; what they also show is his lack of love and empathy towards his daughter and it is this failure that in the end destroys passion and life.

It is not only the father's lack of empathy with his daughter that brings this drama to a tragic end, it also highlights a more general conflict that a child can experience when it has 'two mothers' from different social and economic backgrounds. Juliet's marriage to Romeo represented love, which she had learned from her Nurse. But the Nurse's economic and social dependency upon Juliet's parents meant that she, the Nurse, had no 'natural rights' to state what she believed was best for Juliet.[4] She had to act against the best interests of Juliet because of her social and economic powerlessness. She was put into a position where the values of love, the ones that are the most important for the continuation of creative life, were negated by stronger political forces.

The imaginative portrait of this heroic figure of the Nurse, who gives up so much of her own family life for the welfare of a more privileged child, is heart-rending and yet at the same time evokes feelings of dismay. Why did she let Juliet down? Why could she not stand up to Juliet's bullying parents? The character of the Nurse as portrayed by Shakespeare takes us to the moral and emotional heart of a problem that surrounds the life of the wet nurse. On the one hand she gives up so much of her maternal commitment to her own child and becomes the psychological anchor for the infant she nurses and yet on the other hand, politically and socially, this new attachment is seen by those who employ her as not worthy of consideration and she is rendered powerless. The Nurse finds herself in a political No-Man's Land, in which she has given of her best and finds she has lost everything to those who have economic privilege. Has this been the fate of many wet nurses outside the realm of fiction? Is this the heroic sacrifice that has been expected of them?

The idea that the wet nurse inhabits a social and economic No-Man's Land is most vividly highlighted in the historical cases where the wet nurse is not only of a different class but also of a different race. In the late nineteenth century and early twentieth century in the Southern states of the United States many white plantation owners employed black wet nurses for their children, and in tracing some of the shadows a black wet nurse casts upon the psyche of a white child, the issues that were raised in *Romeo and Juliet* can be seen even more clearly.

Jack London (1876–1916) was born in San Francisco in 1876 and had a black wet nurse, Virginia Prentiss. Prentiss was an African-American who had been born a slave in the Southern states. She had been separated from her mother as a small child and sold into a white household. During the Civil War (1861) when the Union troops sacked the plantation where she worked, she and her mistress fled to Saint Louis. Here she married a 'quadroon', that is to say, a man who was three quarters white. He had fought bravely in the Civil War, as an officer, but when it was discovered that his mother was a mulatto he was discharged, for he was suddenly seen as 'black'.[5] They moved to San Francisco. She had two children and then gave birth to a still-born son on the same day as Jack London's mother, Flora Chaney, gave birth to Jack and here their paths crossed.

Flora Chaney was an unmarried and unstable woman, who had already tried to kill herself twice while pregnant. Jack's father had abandoned her and she was destitute and full of shame at bearing an illegitimate child. She called Jack her 'badge of shame' and turned away from him in disgust when he was born (Haley, 2010: p. 12). But due to the enlightened thinking of Flora's doctor, Jack was rescued from this potential disaster. The doctor saw Flora's distaste for her son and suggested Jack should be 'farmed out' to Virginia Prentiss, whom he knew had just given birth to a still-born son.

Jack was taken into Prentiss' household and breast fed. It is possible that he only stayed there for the first six months of his life, for Flora soon married John London, and Jack was taken back by Flora and had his name changed to London. But however long Jack stayed with Prentiss, she was a good and loving wet nurse and he came to represent her lost son. She referred to him affectionately all her life as her 'white pickaninny' or her 'cottonball' while he called her 'Mammy Jennie' (Haley, 2010: pp. 13–14). There is no indication that Prentiss ever took on other nurslings and so Jack remained in a unique position in her emotional life, and for Jack she was the 'good mother' his own mother failed to be. What effect did this black/white relationship have for both of them? Did their racial differences have any meaning for either of them? And here a nice twist unfolds.

Prentiss brought to the relationship with Jack a legacy of her own slavery and the slavery of her ancestors. She had been born a slave and separated from her mother and sold to a white mistress. But she had become a free woman following the Civil War and her life undoubtedly became better when she reached San Francisco with her husband. However the man she married also carried a complicated ancestral history of slavery. His father had been white and his mother had been half white so legally he was black. However his paternity would have remained unacknowledged for it was an exceptional white man who would look after his 'coloured' and illegitimate children (Smith, 1961). So Prentiss' husband was to see himself as 'black', even though he was 'light-skinned'. This background history of both Prentiss and her husband is important if we are to understand Prentiss' confident assertion that from 'what she had observed of white people and the black experience . . . black people were superior' (Haley, 2010: p. 13). Indeed they were, if we consider the treatment Prentiss and her husband had known. But Prentiss' belief in her superiority may also, quite rightly, have been a reflection upon her capacity to mother Jack, while Flora was so encased in her own neurosis she could never see Jack as more than 'her badge of shame'.

It is a relief to discover that Prentiss, unlike Shakespeare's fictional Nurse, saw black people as superior to those white people who employed her and was able to assert her own strength and power over Jack's mother. Shakespeare has helped us to imagine the potential tragic consequences that followed from the bullying tactics of Juliet's parents, but what effect did Prentiss' belief in her superiority to white women have upon her white nursling Jack? Prentiss and her family stayed close to Jack all his life, indeed they moved twice to be near him, so it is not surprising to discover that Jack maintained a loving devotion to her throughout his life. When he was 15 and wanted to set up his own business as an oyster catcher/poacher she lent him money. In return when Jack became a successful writer he bought her a home and in his will he made sure that she was properly looked after for the rest of her life. It would be safe to say that Prentiss held the most important place in Jack's early emotional life for she was after all his 'first mother' in all but name.

It is impossible to know whether Jack was suddenly weaned from Prentiss' breast when his mother married and he was returned home. But even if it was sudden and traumatic, it was tempered by the fact that Prentiss never completely left him. She was a constant presence whom he could turn to throughout his life. However when we turn to Jack's adult emotional life, a more complicated picture emerges. He must have been strung between 'two mothers' (Hardin, 1985), one black and one white. And this may be reflected in the difficulty he had throughout his life in committing himself to the person he really loved. He fell in love with a Russian refugee, Anna Strunsky, but married a woman he did not love, Bessie Wadden. He had a passionate relationship with a man, George Sterling, whom he believed was his soulmate, but ultimately he ended that relationship. And finally, as we saw with both Rousseau and Talleyrand, he found it difficult to inhabit the role of a father and neglected his two daughters (Haley, 2010).

Can we hear in these unfulfilling and tormenting relationships the echo of his passionate attachment to his wet nurse, Virginia Prentiss, that could never find a comfortable resolution?

And here there are resonances to Juliet's fictional relationship with her wet nurse. Juliet had an emotional mother, her Nurse, and a 'second mother', who represented the cultural values of the time. The values were irreconcilable and Juliet died. Was London strung between two mothers whose values he could not reconcile? It would have been impossible for Jack to have had a relationship with a black woman at the beginning of the twentieth century, for in spite of the American Civil War and the abolition of slavery, the US was still culturally and politically segregated between those who were black and those who were white. There is nothing in the accounts of Jack's life that suggests he ever consciously desired a black woman, but the idea that Jack may have had such a forbidden wish is supported by the autobiographical experience of another white child, Lilian Smith (1897–1966), who was raised by a black nurse.

Smith was a privileged white woman, 20 years younger than Jack, and born in the Southern state of Georgia. She believed passionately that if a white child was nursed and succoured by a black wet nurse this led to a sexual conflict that ate into the hearts of these children. How could a white child nursed at the 'warm deep breast' and 'dark velvety skin' of their coloured nurse, 'not experience an emotional split between the values of the white society who saw the black woman as inferior, and their own deep love for these supposedly less than human people?' (Smith, 1961: p. 127).

In 1949 Smith described, in *Killers of the Dream,* the emotional conflict that she and many other white children experienced between these black wet nurses whose 'warm soft breasts [made one] almost believe in the coloured folks' heaven' in contrast to the 'hopelessness we believed in the white folks' hell' (Smith, 1961: p. 112). It was not surprising to learn that one solution to this split between 'heaven' and 'hell' was that white boys who had had a black wet nurse 'found it natural to seek in adolescence and adulthood a return to this profoundly pleasing experience . . . a tender, passionate, deeply satisfying relation which he was often faithful to, despite cultural barriers' (p. 128). And of course, one unacknowledged result, as in the case of Prentiss' husband, was that in the Southern states there were six million mixed race children, in the middle of the twentieth century, whose fathers denied their paternity (Smith, 1961).

The conflict for girls who had been raised by a black wet nurse made the relationship with their mothers complicated in a different way. Smith certainly does not cite white girls in adolescence having affairs or having children with black youths. But their difficulties were more subtle and silent. In the first place, their mothers were humiliated and deeply ashamed to witness their children more passionately attached to their black nurses. This in turn led to the girl, as Smith described her own experience, to 'close the doors' on the 'passionate love I felt for her [my black Mammy] . . . and instead [give] a half-smiled affection similar to that which one feels for one's dog. I knew but I never believed it, that the deep respect I felt for her, the tenderness, the love, was a childish thing which every normal child outgrows.' In an agonized ending to this paragraph she writes, '"my old mammy" one of the profound relationships of my life. I learned the bitterest thing a child can learn: that the human relations I valued most were held cheap by the world I lived in' (Smith, 1961: pp. 28–9).

If Virginia Prentiss and Lilian Smith are to be believed, black wet nurses brought a 'folk's heaven' to their nursing capacity. In other words, the mothering that Prentiss brought to London and Smith's black nurse brought to her was felt to be superior. They, like Shakespeare's fictional Nurse in *Romeo and Juliet*, knew what was best for the infant they suckled. But the downside was that such a child would have to contend with two mothers, one who evoked the deepest feelings of love, and another who inculcated the cultural values that the child was to live by. What Smith's account also shows is that a white child with a black wet nurse or black nanny has a more transparent sexual conflict; witness the six million mixed race children in the Southern states of America that existed when Smith wrote her book in 1949.

In 1923 Freud was visited in Vienna by an American psychiatrist called Clarence Oberndorf (1882–1954), who came to him for an analysis. Oberndorf had been brought up in the Southern States of the US and had been nurtured by a much loved black wet nurse. In *An Autobiographical Sketch* (1958), which was published posthumously and privately, Oberndorf described his early childhood. He grew up in Selma, Alabama where his father, Joseph, was a prosperous merchant. Joseph was a German Jew who had emigrated with his family to the US in 1859. Joseph married the sister of Oscar Hammerstein, and Oberndorf describes his mother as not unlike her famous brother, 'unpredictable, versatile, and restless' (Kubie, 1954: p. 547). Oberndorf was the youngest of six children, two of whom had died at birth. He was born following an arduous labour and nearly died. His life was saved by a doctor who applied forceps but the result of the forceps delivery was that Oberndorf's skull was crushed. He suffered necrosis of the bone on both sides of his skull and was afflicted with scars all his life. He could not raise his head for a year but he attributed his survival to the devotion of his black wet nurse.

Oberndorf's father died when Oberndorf was 11 and his family moved north. There he went to Cornell Medical School and went on to study neurology and psychiatry and then psychoanalysis. He became a charter member of the New York Psychoanalytic Society in 1911 and then a member of the American Psycho-analytic Association. At that time it was beginning to be clear that in order to become a psychoanalyst one needed to have a personal analysis and so after the First World War he went to Vienna to be analysed by Freud. The analysis lasted five months and ended acrimoniously and with great anger on the part of Freud. There are conflicting accounts of the failure of Oberndorf's analysis with Freud.

On Oberndorf's account, he said that he took a dream to Freud, in the opening hour of his analysis, in which,

> I was on the driver's seat of an old-fashioned country wagon drawn by a white horse and a black horse. From this Freud made the inference that my life had unconsciously been under the influence of two fathers, a white father Joe, and black father Joe, our Negro coachman who had been a slave but who taught me many things beside currying a horse and riding bareback.
>
> (Ginsberg, 1999: p. 244)

Oberndorf disagreed with Freud's interpretation of the dream and they never resolved their disagreement. Oberndorf believed that the influences of his Southern childhood stretched beyond these two men, and he was surely including his wet nurse when he wrote, 'The memories of all these early years reside, or rest or linger vividly in this Southern atmosphere, coloured in both senses by the Negroes of the household, to whom one habitually resorted for solace and advice in childhood troubles' (pp. 243–4).

The second account of Oberndorf's analysis with Freud is given by one of his American colleagues, Abram Kardiner. Kardiner, in his *My Analysis with Freud: Reminiscences* (1977) wrote that Oberndorf had incurred Freud's wrath. It occurred over their disagreement about the meaning of the dream that Oberndorf had described at the beginning of his analysis. According to Kardiner, Freud had not said that Oberndorf had been under the influence of two fathers, Freud had said that he would never marry because he did not know whether to choose between a white woman or a black one. Kardiner continues that it was this 'weak spot' that had infuriated Oberndorf and he and Freud haggled over the meaning of the dream for the remaining months until Freud told him to go. Kardiner ends this second-hand account with the following sentence: 'Freud was unequivocal in his condemnation of Oberndorf's character and of his ability and later on he even refused to write a preface for a book he had written' (Ginsberg, 1999: p. 244). Oberndorf never married, and so perhaps Kardiner's account of Freud's interpretation of the dream is the correct one. But there are other interesting questions that can be asked about the disagreement between Freud and Oberndorf over the dream.

Gay (1988) commented on Freud's analysis of Oberndorf, 'Freud permitted himself an insensitivity he would have found uncivilized in others and, had he analyzed it, symptomatic in himself'. In particular, Freud called Oberndorf ' "the worst" among them [other Americans he was analyzing at the same time]. "He appears to be stupid and arrogant" ' (pp. 564–5). But was he? In Oberndorf's obituary he was described as a man who was more interested in the psychotherapeutic process rather than metapsychology, which might well have annoyed Freud.[6] A further difference was that Oberndorf was passionate about relieving suffering, and he set up psychiatric units in such hospitals as Mount Sinai and helped to organise other psychotherapeutic services for children and for Jews. Perhaps most tellingly, during the last 12 years of his life, he became concerned to understand the reasons for therapeutic failure! (Kubie, 1954). So was Freud's insensitivity to Oberndorf symptomatic of something else?

Freud analysed another American, Smiley Blanton, in the late 1920s, who had also been brought up in the South, though this time he was a not a Jew but a

Presbyterian. Blanton (1971) in his *Diary of My Analysis with Sigmund Freud*, records that 'At one point during the hour, Freud asked me if Jews were not put in the same category as Negroes. I said I had not met with this comparison. Freud said "I often have!"' Does the clue to Freud's anger with Oberndorf lie in those words, 'I often have'? In other words when Oberndorf and Freud disagreed about the interpretation of the dream about the black and the white horse, was it a confrontation between two men, a Jew and the son of a slave owner? When Oberndorf disagreed with Freud, did Freud feel he, a Jew, was being put down like a Negro slave by a white slave owner? Is this what made him so angry?[7]

Does all this really matter? It is, after all, only conjecture and the possible dynamics between them can only be surmised. However, keeping in mind the question about why the wet nurse has not been of interest in psychoanalytic thinking, this row may have helped to obscure a discussion that needed to be held. What was never meaningfully explored was the effect that Oberndorf's black wet nurse had upon Oberndorf's mature sexual desires.[8] And instead we have been left with an unexplored transference/countertransference enactment around a crucially important subject, namely, what effect does the wet nurse have upon the psychological/sexual development of the child she suckles?

The conflict between Freud and Oberndorf also highlights an emotionally complex issue around race, another important issue that has lain dormant in psychological thinking until quite recently (Suchet, 2007).[9] Oberndorf, London and Smith all had good and loving relationships with their black wet nurses but these relationships posed a social and sexual dilemma for them when they grew into adulthood in their racially divided societies. They will have had two models of maternal care: a 'good' mother who fed them and who held them and comforted them and a 'bad' mother, who, in the words of Oberndorf, might have been 'unpredictable, versatile and restless'. They will have struggled with the experience of 'a second mother', who will have been seen as inferior, whether due to class or race, and who, in the interstices of their heart, they may have wished to take as a model for their 'first wife'.

There is another important feature in the relationship that all infants will have had with their wet nurse. They will have imbibed unconscious communications from her. The possible permutations are of their very nature difficult to determine, but at the very least the infant suckled at the breast of a 'milk mother' will pick up unconscious communications that will necessarily be very different from those of the infant's own mother. Prentiss, quite rightly, believed she was a superior mother to Jack London's real mother, Flora Chaney, and this knowledge Jack London will have picked up unconsciously. But how will he have integrated this experience against the backdrop of a culture that believed black women were inferior to white ones?

There has been increasing evidence since the important work of Fraiberg (1987) on the powerful influence of the unconscious mind of the mother upon her baby.[10] This is not a new psychological insight; in the second millennium BC Homer suggested that Achilles was suckled at the breast of his mother, but she 'nurtured him in wrath'. In other words Achilles' aggressive nature was linked to his mother's attitude of mind towards him.[11] However the more recent observations on the effect that the maternal mind has upon the child she nurtures helps to confirm the idea that the wet nurse must therefore be a significant psychological figure within the psyche of the child she nurses. This would challenge the maternal ideal and would significantly shift Freud's belief in the mother's influence. He wrote, 'Children learn to feel for other people . . . a love which is on the model of, and a continuation of, their relation as sucklings to their nursing mother' (Freud, 1905d). The new model would need to include the wet nurse who may become the internalized 'nursing mother'.

In looking at both the literary accounts of the wet nurse and her description in biography and autobiography, a more socially complex picture of her has emerged. She has been imagined as a warm, mature and loving woman, in the fictional accounts of Shakespeare and Dickens, and we are led to believe she became the primary attachment figure to her nurslings. We are also asked to imagine that the break-up of this important relationship left a desolate inner landscape. In the lives of London, Smith and Oberndorf they were left with confusion about the meaning of tender loving care and where to place their trust. What has been so striking is that in spite of literary and biographical evidence the wet nurse has lain in obscurity in our social and psychological history. The opening quotation from Dickens perhaps helps to give a partial answer. The wet nurse's emotional significance may have been undermined by the belief that she was no more than a servant whose employment was 'a mere matter of bargain and sale'. What also seems clear from these literary and biographical accounts of the wet nurse is that the social, psychological and political demands that were made upon her confirm she has had to carry a heavy burden.

Notes

1. 'A mere matter of bargain and sale' (Dickens, 1844 [1948]: p. 29).
2. Dickens' imaginative depiction of the complex emotions surrounding the employment of a wet nurse may have been prompted by the employment of wet nurses for his first two children. His wife seems to have suffered from what today is called 'postnatal depression' and to the distress of Dickens and Catherine, his wife, she found herself unable to breast feed her first two children (Tomlin, 2011).
3. The London Lying-In Hospitals became a well-known source for obtaining wet nurses, after the first one was built in 1747 (Fildes, 1988).
4. It was not until 1951 that the World Health Organization published Bowlby's *Child Care and the Growth of Love*. Subsequently the United Nations, in its post-war Declaration of Human Rights, added, 'A child of tender years shall not be, save in exceptional circumstances, be separated from its mother' (quoted in Brendon, 2005: p. 214).
5. The concept of mulatto was derived from the Spanish word for mule (Davies, 1970).
6. Joan Riviere writing about her analysis with Freud complained, 'He was much more interested in the work in general, than in me as a person. . . . He would as soon as one came in be quite prepared to show me a German letter and discuss it with me, . . . and argue . . . I was also frustrated and deprived because he practically

devoted the whole session to business' (Borch-Jacobsen and Shamdasani, 2012: p.182).

7. Roazen (1975) wrote, 'Whenever Freud sounds intolerant it is likely that something in him was threatened' (p. 251). See also Ashplant (2012) 'As a "black man" with a white mask, Freud internalized racial, gendered, sexual, and familial ideologies, which he both projected onto a range of Others (*Ostjuden,* women, homosexuals, primitives), but also sought to transform by universalizing them' (p. 39).

8. Laplanche (2009) comes near to this possibility in his theory that the unconscious influence of the adult caretaker's own 'slumbering infantile sexuality' (p. 530) may lodge in the unconscious of the child she nurses.

9. See also Davids (2012) and Fletchman-Smith (2011), who have confronted racism in psychoanalytic practice.

10. See also Jones (2006); Stern (1985); and Trevarthen (2008).

11. 'Oh that woman that cannot make her fault her husband's occasion, let her never nurse her child herself, for she will breed it like a fool' (Shakespeare, 1599 [1994]. Act 4, Scene 1).

References

Ashplant, T.G. (2012) Freud, fin-de-siecle politics, and the making of psychoanalysis. In: *History and Psyche: Culture, Psychoanalysis and the Past*, S. Alexander and B. Taylor (eds). New York: Palgrave Macmillan.

Blanton, M.G. (1971) Biographical notes and comments. In: *Diary of My Analysis with Sigmund Freud*, S. Blanton (ed.). New York, N.Y.: Hawthorne Books.

Borch-Jacobsen, M. and Shamdasani, S. (2012) *The Freud Files: An Inquiry into the History of Psychoanalysis.* Cambridge: Cambridge University Press.

Bowlby, J. (1951) *Maternal Care and the Growth of Love.* Geneva: World Health Organization; London: Her Majesty's Stationery Office. Abridged version: *Child Care and the Growth of Love* (2nd edn, 1965). Harmondsworth: Penguin.

Brendon, V. (2005) *Children of the Raj.* London: Phoenix, Orion Books.

Davids, M.F. (2011) *Internal Racism: A Psychoanalytic Approach to Race and Difference.* London: Palgrave Macmillan.

Davies, D.B. (1970) *The Problem of Slavery in Western Culture.* London: Penguin Books.

Dickens, C. (1844) *Dombey and Son.* London: Thomas Nelson.

Fildes, V. (1988) *Wet Nursing: A History from Antiquity to the Present.* Oxford: Basil Blackwell.

Fletchman-Smith, B. (2011) *Transcending the Legacy of Slavery: A Psychoanalytic View.* London: Karnac.

Fraiberg, S. (1987) *Selected Writings,* L. Fraiberg (ed.). Columbus, O.H.: Ohio State University Press.

Freud, S. (1905d) *Three Essays on the Theory of Sexuality.* S.E.5. London: Hogarth Press.

Gay, P. (1988) *Freud: A Life for Our Time.* London; Melbourne: J.M. Dent & Sons.

Ginsberg, L.M. (1999) Freud's racial vocabulary and related fragments from analyses of Clarence B Oberndorf and Smiley Blanton. *International Forum of Psychoanalysis* 8: 243–8.

Haley, J.L. (2010) *Wolf: The Lives of Jack London.* New York: Basic Books.

Hardin, H.T. (1985) On the vicissitudes of early primary surrogate mothering. *Journal of American Psychoanalytic Association* 33: 609–29.

Jones, A. (2006) Levels of change in parent-infant psychotherapy. *Journal of Child Psychotherapy* 32(3): 295–311.

Kardiner, A. (1977) *My Analysis with Freud: Reminiscences.* New York, N.Y.: Norton.

Kubie, L.S. (1954) Clarence P. Oberndorf, M.D. 1882–1954. *Journal of American Psychoanalytic Association* 2: 546–52.

Laplanche, J. (2009) Inzest und infantile Sexualität. *Psyche – Zeitschrift für Psychoanalyse* 63: 525–39.

Malcolm, J. (1982) *Psychoanalysis: The Impossible Profession.* London: Pan Books.

Oberndorf, C.P. (1958) *An Autobiographical Sketch.* Ithaca, N.Y.: Cornell University Infirmary & Clinic.

Pinchbeck, I. and Hewitt, M. (1969) *Children in English Society*, Vols 1 & 2. London: Routledge & Kegan Paul.

Roazen, P. (1975) *Freud and His Followers.* New York: Knopf.

Shakespeare, W. (1595) [1994] *Romeo and Juliet.* London: Penguin Popular Classics.

Shakespeare, W. (1599) [1994] *As You Like It.* London: Penguin Popular Classics.

Smith, L. (1961) *Killers of the Dream.* New York; London: W.W. Norton.

Stern, D.N. (1985) *The Interpersonal World of the Child: A View from Psychoanalysis and Developmental Psychology.* London: Basic Books.

Suchet, M. (2007) Unravelling whiteness. *Psychoanalytic Dialogue* 17: 667–886.

Tomlin, C. (2011) *Charles Dickens: A Life.* London: Penguin Books; Viking.

Trevarthen, C. (2008) Thought in motion. Interdisciplinary approaches to mind and body. Lecture at Tavistock Centre. 5–6 September. New York: Analytic Press.

Chapter 5

Freud and Klein

A complicated psychological picture about the wet nurse emerges from the examples of Jack London, Lilian Smith and Clarence Oberndorf. They all seem to have been strung between competing emotional connections to their mothers and their wet nurses, and this may have been one of the reasons that their later relationships proved complicated. The case of Oberndorf makes transparent the emotional conflict that can be engendered when there is a racial divide between wet nurse and nursling. But all infants who have had two mothers from different classes and cultures are faced with the same question as to where their emotional and sexual loyalties lie; or to put it in another way, having two mothers, from different classes or races, complicates sexual identity and desire.

Psychoanalytic theory has been reluctant to imagine the psychological implications of having two mothers within the internal world. Freud acknowledged that his nurse had left her 'impression', but the nature of this 'impression' remained opaque. However if we take what Freud has written about his early life as a text, we may be able to understand further why the nurse or nanny has had an insignificant place in the Freudian theory of the infant mind.

Freud's nurse left suddenly when he was two and a half, though there is no established evidence that she was his wet nurse. Vitz (1988) wrote, 'It is not entirely clear in the relevant texts whether the nanny was a wet nurse . . . Freud did describe her with the word *Amme* . . . A German word for a nurse for very young children . . . [or] . . . wet nurse' (p. 7). Pinker (1997) suggested that she probably was his wet nurse in the light of Freud's sexualisation of his relationship with his mother. Freud (1900a) however, in an interpretation of his dream about the three Fates, writes that his mother gave him his first nourishment (p. 204). How long she fed him for is not known, but it is unlikely he was breast fed by his mother for many weeks, for she gave birth to his brother Julius when Freud was 11 months old, on one account (Jones, 1953), or when Freud was 17 months old, by another (Gay, 1988), and as has already been suggested fertility is diminished during breast feeding (Fildes, 1988). What is known is that Freud employed a wet nurse for his eldest daughter, Mathilde, which suggests wet nursing must have been a familiar way of nurturing children for both Freud and his wife Martha (Freud, 1961).

The accounts of the nurse's exact role in the care of Freud's early life differ,[1] although Freud himself said she had been his nurse from his earliest infancy (Freud, 1901b). She was Czechoslovakian and a Roman Catholic but her social position has been debated, that is to say, it has been suggested she was the Freuds' landlady. It is generally agreed that she was suddenly dismissed from her care of Freud and sent to prison by Freud's half brother Philipp for supposedly stealing money and toys from Freud.[2] It is not hard to imagine that this sudden dismissal would have a traumatic effect as it came at a very difficult moment in Freud's life. His younger brother Julius had died a few months before, his mother's brother Julius had also just died and his mother was in bed giving birth to his sister Anna.[3] It is not surprising that Freud's own self-analysis did not reveal to him the extent of his despair at the loss of his nurse. Freud himself pointed out that there are some feelings that self-analysis cannot reveal, for they are after all in the unconscious mind.[4] However, Freud did recall his nurse well enough to poignantly write to Fliess (Masson, 1985), 'I shall be grateful to the memory of the old woman who provided me at such an early age with the means for living and going on living. As you see the old liking is breaking through again' (Masson, 1985: p. 269).

At this moment of his self-analysis Freud was faced with a painful memory of his nurse. He remembered 'he was crying in despair' at the time of her dismissal. He was with his half brother Philipp, who had sacked his nurse, and Philipp had jokingly opened a cupboard door to show Freud that his mother was not there. Philipp liked jokes and was playing on the word, *Kasten,* meaning box or closet, though in slang it also means 'put in a box', that is to say, jail (Breger, 2000; Hardin, 1988a, b). The explanation Freud gave for his despair was that he feared his mother had disappeared. However, she walked into the room, 'slender and beautiful' and he was comforted (Masson, 1985: p. 222).

Freud believed his despair reflected his anxiety that his mother might disappear: 'I was afraid she had vanished from me, just as the old woman had a short time before' (Masson, 1985: p. 272). A lot can hang on the way one understands that sentence. It could be said that his anxiety that his mother had disappeared had been aroused by the fact that his nurse had suddenly gone. In other words, the disappearance of his nurse was the primary anxiety that in turn precipitated his fear that his mother might also leave him. But Freud was firmly convinced that the loss of his mother was primary and as a result his nurse was boxed into a cupboard in his mind and she became no more than an 'old' and 'ugly' woman, whose 'impression' he could not fathom. But in spite of Freud's belief that his nurse had been safely put out of mind, an unconscious memory of her does break through from time to time. For instance, when Freud was 16 he returned to his old home-town of Freiberg, where he and his family had lived for the first three years of his life and where he had been looked after by his nurse. He stayed with family friends. In a letter that Freud wrote to his school friend Silberstein he describes Mrs Fluss in the following way:

You should also see how she brought up her seven children and how she is still bringing them up; how they obey her, the older ones more than the younger ones, how no concern of any of the children ceases to be hers. Other mothers – and why hide the fact that ours are among them; we shall not [love] them any the less for it – only look after the physical needs of their sons. Their spiritual development has been taken out of their hands . . . Frau Fluss knows no sphere that is beyond her influence . . . She obviously recognizes that I always need encouragement to speak or to help myself, and she never fails to give it. This is where her dominion over me shows; as she guides me, so I speak.

(Clark, 1980: p. 26)

Later Freud was to write about his nurse in similar terms. As we have seen above, he described her as a woman who had given him not only physical care, but also a 'reason for living'. More than that, in 1897 he wrote to Fliess that his nurse was 'an ugly, elderly but clever woman who told me a great deal about God and hell and gave me a high opinion of my own capacities' (Masson, 1985: p. 219). She was, it seems, a woman, like Mrs Fluss, who was interested in his spiritual development. This is confirmed in the same letter when he says he had asked his mother about her and she told him that his nurse was 'an elderly woman, very shrewd indeed. She was always taking you to church. When you came home you used to preach, and tell us all about how God conducted His affairs' (Masson, 1985: p. 221).

The 'impression' that his nurse had had upon him continued to puzzle Freud; she had given him a reason for living and had given him spiritual guidance; but what was impossible for him to get access to was the unconscious trauma that her sudden disappearance had caused him. Recent ideas taken from attachment theory help us to see why this was so difficult for Freud to grasp, not least because a self-analysis cannot reveal one's own unconscious mind to oneself. Attachment theory suggests that any child who is suddenly separated from its principal caretaker suffers some degree of trauma (Trevarthen, 2008) and furthermore this separation trauma will be hard to integrate or even remember (Jones, 2006). It therefore seems highly likely that Freud suffered a trauma when his nurse left suddenly, but this trauma would have been difficult to access or understand. One consequence has been that Freud was left with no more than a vague 'impression' of her in his mind and as a result the nurse has not figured as a significant person in Freudian psychoanalytic theory.

What is interesting is that Freud's failure to find a significant place for his nurse in his emotional life has been corroborated by the popular prejudice that has accompanied the nurse throughout the history of child-care. It is not only Freud who has seen the nurse as elderly and sexually unattractive and therefore no threat to the 'slender and beautiful' mother. There has been a cultural taboo in imagining the significance of the wet nurse or nanny more generally. Freud may help us to understand a further feature of this taboo. He described his nurse as a robber or thief of his money and toys. But was she? Leaving aside the possibility that this was a trumped up charge made by Philipp,[2] it surely could be said that a much loved surrogate mother could be seen as having 'stolen' the natural affections that a child would have had towards its mother. This is where the angry and negative feelings towards the 'second mother', who has disappeared, find their expression and find their way into negative ideas about delegated mothering. She is no more than a robber who can be despised and dethroned from her position of importance. But there is a poignancy in this idea of the delegated mother being seen as a robber or thief that stretches beyond the disputed fact of the matter. It conjures up images of the child in a bleak landscape of loss that is similar to the No Man's Land inhabited by the wet nurse. In such a situation the child will be left in a state of great anxiety. Who or where is there a reliable person who loves them? Doubt will then be cast upon the reliability of the mother, who up until this point has been no more than a shadowy figure of attachment. The loss of a primary caretaker who is not the mother leaves an indelible scar. Even more painful to acknowledge is that, in such cases, a warm relationship between the mother and child is seldom restored. On all accounts, Freud was never close to his mother.

The idea that a second or surrogate mother might come between the natural affection of mother and child is one that has been hotly debated. But even more challenging is the knowledge that the child might never feel deeply attached or affectionate towards its mother. Perhaps one of the most striking examples of the difficulty in thinking about the emotional consequences of having a second mother is to be seen in the work of Melanie Klein (1882–1960). Anyone familiar with her work will know the central importance she gives to the maternal breast. But what is less well known is that Klein never experienced the maternal breast herself; she was fed by a wet nurse, unlike her three older siblings. She was told by her mother Libussa that 'she was not expected', or perhaps more truthfully, she was not wanted, and this was the reason for her being fed by a wet nurse. However Klein dismissed the emotional significance of having a wet nurse in a few sentences in her unpublished autobiography (Grosskurth, 1985). 'I have no particular feeling that I resented this because there was a great deal of love towards me.' And then she added that her wet nurse 'fed me any time I asked for it'. That is all, and in the next sentence, as though this might console her for the loss of her mother, she elliptically commented, 'At this time Truby King had not done his devastating work' (p. 10).

The fact that Klein made light of this experience, and that by implication she was not 'devastated' by having a wet nurse, does not mean that she was unaffected by the knowledge that her mother had not fed her whereas her siblings had known their mother's breast. Nevertheless, tracing these repercussions is necessarily conjectural. It is not clear from Grosskurth's biography how long Klein's wet nurse fed her. Klein said she could remember her wet nurse feeding her 'any time she asked' (Grosskurth, 1985: p. 10), which suggests Klein must have been at least two before she was weaned, for on Schore's (2002) account memory is not laid down until the second or third year of life.

In trying to imagine the effect that Klein's wet nurse may have had upon her emotional development, it is necessary to turn to the two concepts of Kleinian (1957) theory that have caused most disagreement. She believed that we all come into the world filled with innate envy. 'Envy is an oral-sadistic and anal-sadistic expression of destructive impulses, operative from the beginning of life, and that it has a constitutional basis'. This constitutional envy is driven by the death instinct, with the result that 'hatred is the primary motivating force or instinct towards parents' (p. 176). These powerful sentiments, which seem to carry the weight of Old Testament beliefs, can be more sympathetically reviewed if they are seen as arising from her emotional response to having had 'two mothers' when her siblings had had one.

The tragic and chilling picture of the beginning of life, that 'hatred should be the basis of object-relationships' (Klein, 1932: p. 135), becomes more understandable in the light of the narcissistic hurt that Klein suffered when she was told she was not expected and that unlike her other three siblings she was never proffered the maternal breast. It also helps to make sense of Klein's disinterest in thinking through the biological and evolutionary consequences of holding these two beliefs about innate envy and the death instinct (Polledri, 2012). Klein's belief that an infant comes into the world able to 'phantasise' about its wish to destroy the bounteous breast is not only biologically impossible, for the infant brain does not have such a capacity (Schore, 2002), but it also makes little evolutionary sense to imagine that an infant wishes to destroy life before it has even begun (Darwin, 1872; Bowlby, 1969).

Such a vision does make sense however, *a posteriori*, of an adult trying to understand its unhappiness and anger in childhood.[5] Klein was in a state of acute depression at different stages throughout her life; this depression necessitated long spells away from her children when they were young, and it returned most intensely when her eldest son Hans died in 1934. Her bravest struggle, following in the wake of Hans' death, was to give some developmental structure to a mind beset, as she had been, with so many losses. But what was left out of her struggle to understand her own deep depression was a recognition that her first loss had been the breast of her mother, followed by the loss of the breast of her wet nurse when she was perhaps one or two years old. However, and this is where the controversy lies to this day, her trenchantly held belief that all infants are aggressively wishing to penetrate into their mothers' body and devour the father's penis and the babies inside her, is a phantasmorgoric and highly sexualised vision that bears little correspondence to the capability of the infant mind (Beebe and Latchman, 2002).[6] But such a vision describes well the later confusing distress of a child who is denied the close intimacy with the mother and given another mother instead. Fantasies of wishing to get into the mother's body have often accompanied deprived, unwanted and insecurely attached children (Fraiberg, 1982),[7] and children who have had 'two mothers' are for the most part insecurely attached (Hardin and Hardin, 2000).

One interesting upshot of the split that may take place in the infant mind if it has had two mothers is that there is a tendency to idealise the natural mother, as was the case with both Freud and Klein. This is well described by Klein (1935) when she wrote that she had come across 'some patients . . .[who] turned away from their mother, in dislike or hate, . . . [but] there existed in their minds nevertheless a beautiful picture of the mother' (p. 270). Klein had the insight to see this split in the minds of her patients, but it was impossible for her to imagine that her idealisation of her own mother may have been a response to the confusing and difficult environment she found herself in as a newborn infant with a wet nurse. Klein believed that her mother 'in many ways remained my example and I remember the tolerance she had towards people' (Grosskurth, 1985: p. 65).

The unexplored loss of Klein's wet nurse and before that of her own mother's breast becomes tragically played out when Klein had children of her own. Klein became extremely depressed during each of her three pregnancies, and she allowed herself to be persuaded by her mother, Libussa, after each pregnancy, to leave her children in Libussa's care and spend many months in sanatoriums trying to regain a better mental state. This might seem an enviable solution for a mother who was suffering from postnatal depression, to turn to her mother for help; but Klein and Libussa had a complicated relationship. When Klein was confronted by motherhood Libussa, rather than encouraging Klein to grow into the role, not only took over the maternal role but subtly triumphed over Klein's incapacity. For instance, following the birth of her second child, Hans, Klein collapsed again and left the children with her mother. Libussa was to write on this occasion, when Klein was in a sanatorium for several months, 'Why do you make every minute of your life a misery and forbid yourself any joy because of them? You can completely rest assured! The children could not be any healthier or look better than they do now' (Grosskurth, 1985: p. 50). As Grosskurth pointed out, the hidden message in that letter was surely that Klein's children were doing better without her.

Throughout her life Klein's mother needed to be reassured of her central position in the lives of her children and grandchildren. This is borne out in a letter she wrote to Klein's adored older brother Emmanuel in 1901, when he was in Italy:

> My dear and beloved child, I must tell you that your relationship with Melanie has often filled me with jealousy. Yet in the course of time I just got used to it and resigned myself to it *as I always do*. I believe, dear child, that there is not a bond, be it that of friendship or of love, that is as strong and powerful as that of mother-love.
>
> (Grosskurth, 1985: p. 24. Italics added)

This was the maternal mire that Klein had to struggle against; a mother always interfering in her children's lives in order to maintain her dominance and be reassured she was the most loved.[8] The tragedy was that Klein inflicted as much pain upon her own children as she had suffered, and she became as impossible as Libussa. A heart-felt letter from her daughter Melitta in 1932 reflected Klein's need to dominate her children, though there is one difference – Melitta expressed feelings towards her mother that Klein had never been able to even imagine about her mother; Melitta wrote, 'Unfortunately, you have a strong tendency towards trying to enforce your way of viewing, or feeling, your interests, your friends, etc. onto me' (Grosskurth, 1985: p. 199).

The difficulty in nurturing the next generation has been a feature of some of those who have been fed by a wet nurse, such as Rousseau, Talleyrand and London. So perhaps it is not surprising to discover that Klein also had difficult and complicated feelings about becoming a mother. Klein's maternal intuition, or perhaps it would be more truthful to say lack of maternal empathy, surfaced most clearly when her third child Eric was born. She became even more depressed when she discovered she was pregnant for a third time, as though she could no longer struggle with her conflicts about motherhood. She employed a wet nurse for him, unlike her two other children, Melitta and Hans, and thereby repeated her own experience.[9] She had no conscious awareness, at the time, of what she was doing nor does she seem to have thought that a wet nurse might get between the relationship of a mother and her child. Yet it seems painfully clear that when she decided to analyse Eric, between the ages of three and five, he was suffering from more than a conflict about his sexual fantasies.

In *The Development of the Child* (1921), Klein gives a lengthy account of Eric's analysis. He is called Fritz and Klein says his difficulties are slight, anyway at the beginning; he is a bit slow in talking and cannot master colours or the concept of time or number. Klein encourages his intellectual development and answers his questions about 'where did I come from' with a fearless account of his growth in his mother's tummy. Klein believed his intellectual and investigative impulses developed through her truthful answers to all his questions. But then there was a setback and he became brooding and withdrawn. He began to have nightmares, he turned away from Klein, and became naughtier and disinclined to eat. Klein believed that this was the moment when she needed to enlighten him about procreation.

> I explain that the big motor is his papa, the electric car his mamma and the little motor himself, and that he has put himself between papa and mamma because he would so much like to put papa away altogether and to remain alone with his mamma and do with her what only papa is allowed to do.
>
> (Klein, 1921: p. 35)

Eric, or Fritz, becomes listless and bored and begins to compulsively run to the window 'whenever he heard a vehicle pass and was quite unhappy if he ever missed one' (p. 37). But this poignant moment is seen as a 'play-inhibition'. What is ignored in this compulsive behaviour is the idea that he might be looking for something or someone outside his relationship with his mother.

Eric by the age of five had suffered many losses. His mother had been deeply depressed when he was born and had often been away; he was handed to a wet nurse; he had lost his wet nurse and more recently his grandmother, who had died.

On top of all that, between the ages of two and three, Eric's father was in the war and was absent for a year. Eric was very fond of him, but when Arthur returned at the time of Eric's analysis, it was only briefly, because he had taken a job in Sweden. So when Klein is describing Eric running to the window, his father had just left for Sweden and Klein and Arthur's marriage was breaking up. To add to these losses, they had just moved house and Eric was deeply unhappy at his new school, where he was being bullied and was distressed at the change of environment. None of these painful events, which took place during the first five years of Eric's life, are part of Klein's interpretation of Eric's 'distaste for play' (Klein, 1921: p. 28).

From this reading of both Freud and Klein and the suggestion that they were unaware of the significance of the losses of their surrogate mothers, it seems more generally that what needs to be thought about is the traumatic effect of having two mothers and the conflict it creates in the child's emerging emotional and sexual identity. It is clear from Klein's account of her analysis of Eric that she believes that his emotional difficulties are a result of sexual conflict, but what is not taken into account is that before such subtle fantasies about his wish to get between his mother and father can have any meaning, he needed help in understanding the precarious state of his inner world, with figures fleeing all over the place: a depressed mother who spent long periods in sanatoriums; his father who had gone to war and then returned and disappeared again; a wet nurse who had gone and a grandmother who had recently died. In both Freud and Klein, loss and infant sexuality have been seamlessly run together and in so doing what gets lost is the idea that sexualisation may be a defence against loss (Glasser, 1985). There is no room in the myth of the universality of the Oedipus Complex for two mothers and so one mother has necessarily to be occluded. Freud remembered the *Karsten* was empty and he was in despair but the mother, 'slender and beautiful', walked in and his despair disappeared. But this image of a sexually attractive mother may be an exciting and enticing way of covering over the earlier loss of a surrogate mother.

One of the counter-arguments to this view of Freud and Klein is to remember they were bound by the culture and mores of their time, and an understanding of the trauma of losing a significant caretaker in early life was yet to be recognised and understood in psychoanalytic theory. However Freud had a friend who was acutely aware of the divided loyalty he suffered between his wet nurse and his mother. This was Groddeck (1866–1934), a German physician who practised in Baden-Baden until he fled to Switzerland when Hitler came to power. What made it possible for him to think about his divided loyalties? Was it because he never trained as a psychoanalyst? He was trained as a doctor but he used psychoanalytic ideas in his treatment of medical cases; that is to say, he took what today might be called a 'holistic' view of illness. He suggested that there was a force in us all that he called the 'It' and believed that in illness as in health what is being expressed are different states of the It.

The It is not to be confused with the unconscious; it includes both the conscious and the unconscious and holds absolute sway over the activities of the brain which it has built up. There is no opposition between the ego and the It; rather the ego is a function of the It.

(Groddeck, 1923: pp. 24–5)

His best known book was translated into English in 1935 and was called *The Book of the It*. Freud was impressed by Groddeck's concept of the 'It', and in 1923 when he wrote *The Ego and the Id* he acknowleged that he had taken Groddeck's idea that the 'It' ruled our lives. However Freud did not leave it there and he transformed the idea of the 'It' into a part of the unconscious Ego, namely the Id. In doing so Freud transformed Groddeck's concept of the 'It', and one result has been that Groddeck's concept has been largely forgotten and more importantly the idea of an It that plays a more unified part in the life of man has been lost.

The Book of the It is written as a series of autobiographical letters to a 'fair lady' and signed by Patrik Troll. In the first letter, he tells her of his experience of having a wet nurse. His mother had been unable to breast feed him after contracting an inflammation of the breast while feeding one of his older siblings. She had therefore decided to hire a wet nurse before he was born. However he arrived early and the wet nurse she had taken on was not available for three days and so he was 'scantily nourished by a woman who came twice a day' and he reflects, 'To have to go hungry is not a kind of welcome for a new-born infant' (Groddeck, 1923: p. 6). His wet nurse did eventually arrive and stayed for three years. But the question throughout this first letter is, what did he feel, or what would any other baby feel in the same circumstances? He asks, rhetorically, 'Have you ever pondered over the experiences of a baby who is fed by a wet nurse?' (p. 7). His answer is that,

[t]he matter is somewhat complicated, at least if the child has a loving mother. On the one hand, there is that mother in whose body the baby has lain for nine months, care-free, warm, in undisturbed enjoyment. Should he not love her? And on the other hand, there is that second woman to whose breast he is put every day, whose milk he drinks, whose fresh, warm skin he feels, and whose odour he inhales. Should he not love her? But to which of them shall he hold? The suckling nourished by a nurse is plunged into doubt, and never will he lose that sense of doubt. His capacity for faith is shaken at its foundation, and a choice between two possibilities for him is always more difficult than for other people. And to such a man, . . . [his] emotional life has been divided at the start.

(Groddeck, 1923: pp. 7–8)

Groddeck's account of having a wet nurse may be true for all infants who have had a wet nurse. Their minds are split between two primitive physical experiences that leave them with traces of doubt about the true nature of love and with a difficulty in making choices. This dilemma seems to have been experienced by Jack London, who could not choose the woman he loved, as was also the case of Clarence Oberndorf (see Chapter 4). Groddeck helps to make sense of Oberndorf's conflict between his black wet nurse whom he loved and a mother towards whom he felt indifferent. Groddeck's description also adds another dimension to the angry encounter between Oberndorf and Freud. Perhaps they each unconsciously feared the pain of discovering their losses of a surrogate mother. Freud, Klein, Groddeck and, before them, London, Smith and Oberndorf had been deprived of the experience of 'the mother's loving and giving breast' (Klein, 1945: p. 321), but what none of them, and that includes Groddeck, recognised, was that they had suffered a double loss, both the loss of the mother's loving and giving breast but also the loss of the breast they had been given. It might be added that Klein's two concepts of the 'good breast' and a 'bad breast' reflect not so much an inevitable split that takes place in the infant mind when fed at the breast of its mother but a split that does take place when the infant has two mothers. As Lewin (1953) suggested, 'a depriving mother actually injures the biological and physiological development of the child' and one consequence is that ' "breast" comes to mean darkness and evil' (p. 109). So although Groddeck has helped us see that the infant with two mothers may always be assailed by doubt about the goodness of the world and have difficulty in making choices, what has lain in unexplored territory in the psychoanalytic literature is that a mother who hands her child over to a surrogate mother will usually be subjecting her infant to two losses: the loss of her breast and then the loss of the surrogate mother and her breast.

There have been some psychoanalytic accounts of the possible ill effect that the loss of a surrogate mother might have upon a young child, but they have given a calm reassurance to all mothers by implying the infant will soon get over the loss. For instance, Helen Deutsch (1965) gave an account of the loss of the surrogate mother that her own son Martin suffered. Deutsch, like Klein, published the case as though Martin was a patient and she calls him Rudi. Rudi had been looked after by 'a mother surrogate' for the first two years of his life while Deutsch was working, though she managed to breast feed him for several months by taking him into work and then handing him over to his nurse after feeds (Roazen, 1975). The nurse had to leave when Rudi was two, and she never said goodbye to him. Almost instantly his behaviour regressed. He rejected the new nursemaid and he refused to eat except if his mother fed him. He started to have nightmares and he could not sleep without his mother and he became incontinent. However after nine days of distress Deutsch was quite confident that 'Rudi returned to reality. . . . [he] overcame his first bitter disappointment in a period of nine days. The completion of this task represented a major step in his adjustment to his external environment' (Deutsch, 1965: pp.162–4). Deutsch's confident assertion that Rudi had completely recovered was not borne out by Martin's later development and he and Deutsch had a difficult and distant relationship; as Deutsch was to write, he had a 'murderous hate filled aggression against me' (Roazen, 1975: p. 284).

Deutsch's discussion about the effect that the loss of her son's surrogate mother had upon his state of mind did not awaken much interest in psychoanalytic theory. Perhaps the most memorable contribution to the obliteration of the surrogate mother is to be found in Mahler (1961), who wrote,

> The primitive ego seems to possess an amazing ability to absorb and synthesize complex object images without adverse effect, and on occasion even with benefit. This, the Gestalt of the nurse, who may be relegated to the function of providing immediate need satisfaction, is synthesized with the Gestalt of the mother, who may be available only as an additional or transient ego.
>
> (p. 334)

In the same vein, in 1971, Lisbeth Sachs made a more general comment about 'maids'. Her paper, *The Maid: Her Importance in Clinical Development*, concerned the presence of maids in a child's early life and she argued that a maid can serve as 'a useful purpose in the child's emotional development' (p. 482). And by that she meant that like a therapist the maid can sometimes bear the brunt of the child's rage against the mother and lessen the fierce oedipal battle. From these brief examples there is an emphasis that the child may not be unduly affected when surrogate mothers, nurses or maids leave, or if they do seem to suffer, it is only short lived and they quickly recover from the loss.

This belief, that the infant turns the gestalt of the nurse into the mother, while it may be true in terms of conscious memory, is not borne out by the research that has been carried out by Hardin (1985), who was the first psychoanalyst to investigate the effect that the loss of a surrogate mother may have upon the emotional development of the child. By 2000 his 20-year research led him to several conclusions. If the principal caretaker for the first years of a child's life is someone other than its mother, then that caretaker will become the most important attachment figure for the child. If the caretaker leaves during these early years of attachment the child will suffer a traumatic loss. But this traumatic loss will be too difficult to integrate into the child's mind and will lay hidden and the surrogate mother will be forgotten and, as was the case with Freud, she will be eclipsed by the image of the mother. This, Hardin believes, is an important reason why the surrogate mother has remained unobserved in the psychoanalytic literature.

He suggests that a gap or lack of connection can be felt in the work with adults who have lost a surrogate mother in early childhood. There is a deadness in the therapy and this is followed by a failure to find significant meaning in or attachment to the relationship to the therapist. All too often this stalemate has been seen as a 'negative therapeutic reaction'. However Hardin suggests that behind the affectless relationship between therapist and client lies a deeper and more distressed state of mind that has never been recognised or even noticed. Patients, therapists, as well as parents have believed that the absence of memory in the child of an early surrogate mother confirms the lack of attachment the infant must have had towards her. But Hardin believes that this is a false assumption. A lack of conscious memory does not necessarily mean there was a lack of meaningful connection between a child and an early surrogate mother. This surrogate mother may be 'eclipsed' by a conscious memory of the mother, but underneath the image of the mother may lie another 'second mother' who has failed to find a significant place in the world of psychoanalytic theory but is present in the internal world of the child (Hardin, 1985: p. 1231).

The eclipsing of the surrogate mother by the image of the mother offers a good explanation as to why she is absent in the psychoanalytic literature. But there is another reason why the surrogate mother is relegated to a meaningless place in autobiographical writing and in psychological understanding. The traumatised infant, in its attempt to heal itself creates an idealised and sometimes sexualised image of the mother. This serves to cover over or deny the fragile and often hostile bond between mother and child that has withered in the intervening years of surrogate mothering. In its place, there is, as Klein wrote, a beautiful picture of the mother, which conceals the pain and hostility that has been unwittingly created between mother and child. The child remains distant from its mother for the rest of its life and finds difficulty in ever trusting an intimate relationship again.

Although we may not be able to judge exactly the feeling of 'a nursing babe', thanks to Freud's original belief in the importance of early infantile experience, we have been able to investigate further into the complex feelings that can be aroused in a child whose principal caretaker is a surrogate mother. As Groddeck suggested, in the case where there has been a wet nurse, the infant can be left with a lifelong doubt about the trustworthiness of human relationships.

Notes

1. See Blum (1977); Breger (2000); Gay (1988); Grigg (1973); Hardin (1987, 1988a, b); Jones (2006); Raphael-Leff (1990); Swan (1974); Vitz (1988) for varying accounts of Freud's early life.
2. Krull (1987) has suggested that the reason for the dismissal of Freud's nurse was because Amalia, Freud's mother, and Philipp, Freud's half brother, were having an affair, and they were fearful that the nurse might reveal this to Jacob, Freud's father, and the rest of the family.
3. The time of the dismissal of Freud's nurse is disputed by Vitz (1988), who believes she was dismissed six months after the birth of Anna, and at the time when the Freud family moved first to Leipzig and then to Vienna.
4. It is interesting to note that Freud had a 'lifelong preoccupation with great figures who had two mothers': Oedipus, Moses and Leonardo da Vinci (Vitz, 1988: p. 26).
5. There are 'doubts about the Kleinian psychoanalytic theory that babies are innately full of envy and greed. It seems more likely that a predominance of negative emotions is associated with abnormal experiences of the mother-baby relationship. . . . [I]t is probably more accurate to think of the hostility and envy of the depressed mother towards her baby than vice versa' (Gerhardt, 2004: p. 124).
6. See also Polledri (2012); Schore (2002); and Trevarthen (2008).

7. See also Gerhardt (2004) and Jones (2006).
8. I am grateful to Tanya Stobbs for pointing out the discrepancy between Libussa's desire to control every aspect of her children's lives and the fact that she handed Melanie over to a wet nurse.
9. Klein, however, was to put it the other way round. She believed that 'some mothers are not able to love and enjoy the possession of their children because they feel too guilty of taking, in phantasy, their own mother's place. A woman of this type may not be able to tend her children herself, but has to leave them to the care of a nurse' (Klein, 1935: p. 321).

References

Beebe, B. and Lachman, F. (2002) *Infant Research and Adult Treatment: Co-Constructing Interactions.* Hillsdale, N.J.: Analytic Press.

Blum, H. (1977) The prototype of pre-oedipal construction. *Journal of American Psychoanalytic Association* 25: 757–85.

Bowlby, J. (1969) *Attachment*, Vol. 1. London: Hogarth Press.

Breger, Louis (2000) *Freud: Darkness in the Midst of Vision.* New York; Chichester: John Wiley.

Clark, R.W. (1980) *Freud: The Man and the Cause.* New York: Random House.

Darwin, C. (1872) *Darwin: The Indelible Stamp. Four Essential Volumes in One*, J. Watson (ed.). Philadelphia; London: The Running Press.

Deutsch, H. (1965) A two year old's first love comes to grief. In: *Clinical Psychoanalytic Studies*, J.D. Sutherland (ed.). New York: International University Press.

Fildes, V. (1988) *Wet Nursing: A History from Antiquity to the Present.* Oxford: Basil Blackwell.

Fraiberg, S. (1982) Pathological defenses in infancy. *Psychoanalytic Study of the Child* 51: 612–35.

Freud, S. (1900a) *The Interpretation of Dreams.* S.E.4–5. London: Hogarth Press.

Freud, S. (1901b) *Psychopathology of Everyday Life.* S.E.6. London: Hogarth Press.

Freud, S. (1923b) *The Ego and the Id.* S.E.19. London: Hogarth Press.

Freud, S. (1961) *Letters of Sigmund Freud, 1873–1939,* E.L. Freud (ed.), T. Stern and J. Stern (trans.). London: Hogarth Press.

Gay, P. (1988) *Freud: A Life for Our Time.* London; Melbourne: J.M. Dent & Sons.

Gerhardt, S. (2004) *Why Love Matters: How Affection Shapes a Baby's Brain.* London: Routledge.

Glasser, M. (1985) The weak spot: some observations on male sexuality. *International Journal of Psychoanalysis* 66: 409, 4, 405–15.

Grigg, K.A. (1973) The role of the nursemaid in Freud's dreams. *American Psychoanalytic Association* 21: 108–26.

Groddeck, G. (1923) [1949] *The Book of the It*, V.M.E. Collins (trans.). London: Vision Press.

Grosskurth, P. (1985) *Melanie Klein: Her World and Her Work.* London: Maresfield Press.

Hardin, H.T. (1985) On the vicissitudes of early primary surrogate mothering. *Journal of American Psychoanalytic Association* 33: 609–29.

Hardin, H.T. (1987) On the vicissitudes of Freud's early mothering – 1: Early environment and loss. *Psychoanalytic Quarterly* 56: 628–44.

Hardin, H.T. (1988a) On the vicissitudes of Freud's early mothering – 1i: Alienation from his biological mother. *Psychoanalytic Quarterly* 57: 72–86.

Hardin, H.T. (1988b) On the vicissitudes of Freud's early mothering. –1ii: Freiberg, screen memory and loss. *Psychoanalytic Quarterly* 57: 209–23.

Hardin, H.T. and Hardin, D.H. (2000) On the vicissitudes of early primary surrogate mothering – II: Loss of the surrogate mother and arrest of mourning. *Journal of American Psychoanalytic Association* 48: 1229–58.

Jones, E. (1953) *Sigmund Freud: A Life's Work*, Vols 1–3. London: Hogarth Press.

Jones, A. (2006) Levels of change in parent-infant psychotherapy. *Journal of Child Psychotherapy* 32(3): 295–311.

Klein, M. (1921) [1975] The development of the child. In: *Love, Guilt and Reparation and Other Works. 1921–1945*, pp. 1–54. New York: Delta Books, Dell Publishing.

Klein, M. (1932) [1975] *The Psychoanalysis of Children*. New York: Delta Books, Dell Publishing.

Klein, M. (1935) [1975] A contribution to the psychogenesis of manic -depressive states. In: *Love, Guilt and Reparation and Other Works, 1921–1945*, pp. 262–90. New York: Delta Books, Dell Publishing.

Klein, M. (1945) [1975] The Oedipus complex in the light of early anxieties. In: *Love, Guilt and Reparation and Other Works, 1921–1945*, pp. 370–420. New York: Delta Books, Dell Publishing.

Klein, M. (1957) [1975] Envy and gratitude. In: *Envy and Gratitude and Other Works, 1946–1963*, pp. 176–236. New York: Delta Books, Dell Publishing.

Krull, M. (1987) *Freud and His Father*, A.J. Pomerans (trans.). London: Hutchinson.

Lewin, B.D. (1953) Reconsideration of the dream screen. *Psychoanalytic Quarterly* 22: 174–99.

Mahler, M. (1961) Sadness and grief in childhood. *Psychoanalytic Study of the Child* 16: 332–51.

Masson, J.M. (1985) *The Complete Letters of Sigmund Freud to Wilhelm Fliess, 1887–1904*. Cambridge, M.A.; London: Harvard University Press.

Pinker, S. (1997) *How the Mind Works.* London: Penguin Books.

Polledri, P. (2012) *Envy is Not Innate: A New Model of Thinking.* London: Karnac.

Raphael-Leff, J. (1990). If Oedipus was an Egyptian. *International Review of Psychoanalysis* 17(3): 309–37.

Roazen, P. (1975) *Freud and His Followers.* New York: Knopf.

Sachs, L.J. (1971) The maid: her importance in child development. *Psychoanalytic Quarterly* 40: 469–84.

Schore, A.N. (2002) Advances in neuropsychoanalysis, attachment theory, and trauma research: implications for self psychology. *Psychoanalytic Inquiry* 22: 433–84.

Swan, J. (1974) Mater and Nannie. Freud's two mothers and the discovery of the Oedipus complex. *American Imago* 31: 1–64.

Trevarthen, C. (2008) Thought in motion. Interdisciplinary approaches to mind and body. Lecture at Tavistock. 5–6 September. New York: Analytic Press.

Vitz, P.C. (1988) *Freud's Christian Unconscious.* New York: Guildford Press.

Chapter 6

The nanny[1]

The difficulty in finding the 'impression' of the nurse or wet nurse may be linked to a traumatic effect on the child if the nurse suddenly disappears, as in the case of Freud, and could lead to the memory being blocked out. In the history of the wet nurse the failure to find her impression by social historians, biographers or psychologists seems to reflect a similar repression. Where once she stood there is now a blank space and this is reinforced by a collective – or is it collusive? – wish to deny her emotional importance. The result has been that she is represented within the psychoanalytic literature in the 'retiring manner . . . [she] maintain[s] in the . . . domestic setting' (Hardin and Hardin, 2004: p. 1511).

There has been general agreement that in England by the end of the nineteenth century, the profession of wet nursing had almost died out, because of economic, social, medical and psychological reasons, such as the growth of industrialisation, where work in factories provided women with better and more secure pay. Wet nursing also declined following the pasteurisation of milk and the invention of a satisfactory bottle, while another contributing factor was concern for the child of the wet nurse whose life had often been cut short in a 'baby farm' (Fildes, 1986, 1988). These shifts were also accompanied by a re-evaluation of mothering and motherhood. Mothers were beginning to be seen as 'the guardians of the home and hearth, women were charged with responsibility for the moral health not only of the next generation but of the nation and later on of the Empire' (Hughes, 1993: p. 55). However, the rich and the aspiring middle classes were still faced with the question about the day-to-day care of their children. For instance, there was much pressure upon wealthy middle-class families who aspired to become part of the 'gentry', that they should become 'refined' and 'polite' and that meant that the lady of the household must not be seen to 'touch any article, no matter how delicate, in the way of trade, [or] she loses caste and ceases to be a lady' (Hughes, 1993: pp. 11–13). So the delegation of mothering to a nanny became a necessity for those who were fearful of losing their caste. Some middle-class women did begin to breast feed their babies while at the same time employing nannies to look after the day-to-day care of their child, for 'breast feeding was re-defined as a natural and healthy practice for the responsible middle-class mother' (Nead, 1990: p. 27). However as Gaythorne-Hardy (1993) suggests, it was still exceptional.

He cites an Irish nanny who was employed in Imperial Russia at the end of nineteenth century. She brought up Baroness Budberg but remained in the family and looked after the Baroness' children when they were born. It was said that she [the nanny] 'made her [the Baroness] suckle her son for eleven months' (p. 127).

For the most part the majority of rich women from the late nineteenth century both in England and in many parts of Europe, still preferred to hand over their babies to a nanny who would feed them from birth with a bottle. 'Hundreds of thousands of mothers ... simply abandon[ed] all loving and disciplining and company of their children, sometimes almost from birth, to the absolute care of other women, total strangers, nearly always uneducated, about whose characters they must usually have had no real idea at all' (p. 19.). Even at the end of the twentieth century this practice seems to continue, although now the nanny might be called the housekeeper. A psychoanalyst, Virginia Hunter, comments:

> I notice in my practice, which is basically an upper middle class practice, that more and more women feel entitled to have children despite their primary commitment to their work. They have a child and they get a housekeeper and off they go. And the housekeeper may change many times. They think nothing about the child having a loss.
>
> (1993: p. 3)

In Gaythorne-Hardy's (1993) book, *The Rise and Fall of the British Nanny*, he suggests that from 1850 until 1939, there were probably per annum 'between two hundred and fifty thousand and half a million' nannies in England in a population that 'rose steadily from 32.5 million to approximately 44.8 million' (p. 181). This may suggest that there was only a small proportion of nannies in the total population, but nevertheless nannies were employed by a large number of the upper and aspiring middle classes, though the middle classes may have represented no more than 5 per cent of the total population. How many politicians were influenced by the nursery rules and nanny's strictures? How many artists, separated from their mothers by other carers, suffered the agony that Proust describes when his mother gave him a goodnight kiss?

> This good night lasted for so short a time; she went down again so soon that the moment in which I heard her climb the stairs, and then caught the sound of her garden dress of blue muslin, from which hung little tassels of plaited straw, rustling along the double-doored corridor, was for me a moment of the keenest sorrow.
>
> (1913: p. 10)

A generalised portrait of the nanny in the nineteenth century and up until the mid-twentieth century might be described in the following way. She would be unmarried but she would come from much the same class as the wet nurse; the daughter of a farm worker or industrial worker and in some cases her mother might have been in service. She would not have had the benefit of secondary education and there was no formalised nursery training before the 1920s. She would enter a household, perhaps at the age of 12 or 13, as an under nurse or nursery maid and gradually work her way up through the social hierarchy of the servant world. She would take over the role of nanny when there was a vacancy and nannies usually moved on after four or five years. From the moment she became nanny she would rule the nursery behind a green baize door. Now she would be waited on by under nurses and a cook who would have to send up food specially cooked for her and her children. She would wear a uniform and run the nursery on a strict routine, with toilet training being a significant part of her disciplinarian armour. If, exceptionally, the mother was breast feeding her baby, the nanny would deliver the baby at its regular feed time to the mother and collect it immediately when the feed had ended. She would be expected to wash the baby and take it for walks in the pram and attend to all the baby's other needs.

The more usual routine was that the nanny would have the sole care of the baby from birth, feeding the baby with a bottle, and the mother would become extraneous to her baby's life. Many nannies reported that they could not understand why their employers bothered to have children when they took such little interest in them (Streatfield, 2012). The mother might look in for 10 minutes in the morning to find out about the nanny's plans for the day, and would see the child again in the evening. On this occasion the baby would be changed into its best clothes and taken down to the drawing room and the mother, and the father if he was around, would entertain the baby from about half past four in the afternoon until six o'clock, when it was time for the baby to go to bed. The sole contact that the infant might have with its mother would be for an hour or two a day. Even when it was the nanny's day off or on the few occasions she might take a holiday, a deputy nanny would usually be taken on.

It was exceptional for a nanny to remain in the same household for her lifetime, or to look after the child beyond the age of five when they would go to school or a governess would be employed. 'The bottom fell out of my small safe world' wrote Sybil Lubbock (1939: p. 155) when she returned from a summer holiday to find her nanny had been dismissed and a governess had arrived to take over her care. One exception was nanny Sibley, who was the nanny to Lord Curzon's three daughters. Lady Curzon, their mother, had died when the children were very young and nanny Sibley gave up her life and her fiancé to look after these three motherless children. The eldest daughter, Irene, Baroness Ravensdale was to write, 'The real prop and backbone of my life was our Nanny Sibley. To her I owe – if I possess them at all – the flowering in one of God's gifts of love and kindness to others' (Gaythorne-Hardy, 1993: p. 151). It was more common for a child to have several nannies, especially if the nanny did not get on well with her employer or the mother became jealous of the relationship that was growing between her child and the nanny. Massey's (2006) mother complained once, 'You love Nanny more than you love me' (p. 101). The nanny might also be dismissed when a new sibling arrived and a new nanny would be employed, causing much pain and anger in the older sibling.

The nanny, unlike the wet nurse, has been present in many novels, biographies and autobiographies. In these memoirs we no longer have to imagine the impact that the nanny may have had solely from epitaphs or manuals on child rearing. She is within living memory in the lives of many well known cultural figures and we can sense her unforgotten presence. Lord Shaftesbury's (1801–1883) parents showed little love or affection for him, and writing in an autobiographical fragment at the end of his life he described his mother as 'a dreadful woman' whom he hoped to expunge from his memory. But there was a housekeeper, Maria Millis, who showed him care and affection, and when she died, when Shaftesbury was still a child, she left him her watch, which he wore for the rest of his life, saying that it had been given to him 'by the best friend he ever had in the world' (Turnball, 2011: pp. 15–17). Anna Freud (1895–1982) recalling her nanny said she was 'the oldest and most real relationship of my childhood' (Young-Bruehl, 1989: p. 398) and Leonard Woolf (1880–1969) remembering his nanny and nursery life, wrote:

> I can still feel myself physically enfolded in the warmth and safety of the great nursery . . . the fire blazing behind the tall guard, the kettle singing away and Nurse, with her straight black hair parted in the middle and her smooth, oval peasant face, reading the Baptist Times or the vision of the opium eater [*Confessions of an English Opium Eater* by Thomas de Quincy].
>
> (Gaythorne-Hardy, 1993: p. 124)

Mary Benson (1841–1918), the wife of the Archbishop of Canterbury, E.W. Benson, and mother of the writers A.C. Benson (1862–1925) and E.F. Benson (1867–1940), was brought up by Elizabeth Cooper, a semi-educated Yorkshire woman. It was her presence that provided Mary with 'love, warmth and comfort' whereas she was 'a little frightened of her mother'. Beth's 'love was a solitary beacon of affection' (Bolt, 2012: pp. 3–28). It was to Beth, as she was known, that Mary turned when at 19 she had her first child. Beth came and lived with the Benson family and brought up all of Mary's six children and earned the lasting devotion of them all. A.C. Benson was to write, 'The only real figure was the old nurse', and 'the love I had and have for her is almost the deepest emotion of my life' (Bolt, 2012: pp. 89, 300). E.F. Benson was also to write that 'it was the face of his nurse . . . leaning over his crib . . . with her comforting presence that quite robbed the dark of its terrors' (pp. 89–92).

These children were fortunate for it seems that their nannies remained for a sufficient length of time so that a firm relationship of security was established. There could, however, be a subtle downside to a warm attachment to a nanny. In the memoirs of the actress Anna Massey (1937–2011) she emphatically states, 'Gertrude Burbidge [her nanny] was the mainstay of my life. She had entered our family when my brother Daniel was three weeks old and she stayed with us for the rest of her life' (Massey, 2006: p. 7). She goes on to describe a familiar picture of the child brought up by a nanny: 'Our world in Mother's house centred entirely round the day and night nurseries, where Nanny ruled her kingdom' (p. 7). Gertrude Burbige was not very maternal and was also a strict disciplinarian but her redeeming feature was that she was supremely reassuring and forgave her children everything. Massey's feelings about Gertrude were in contrast to her feelings about her mother who never made her feel safe for she was so seldom there. This insecurity must have been augmented by the absence of a father who had left when she was a year old. Massey could not bear to be parted from her nanny and would cry inconsolably when she took a day off or went on holiday. It seems that although Massey's nanny was the mainstay of her life, Massey suffered throughout her life from a feeling of insecurity for 'Nanny of course . . . did not have the knowledge to assuage the deeper fears and neuroses that were developing in me' (p. 25). When Massey grew up, married and had a son, nanny came and lived with her. Massey's own marriage broke down soon after the birth of her son and so mother and son became 'her [nanny's] two charges' (p. 101). But when nanny died of cancer a few years later Massey had a breakdown. 'Her death was like losing two parents on the same day . . . Everything fell apart. . . . There was a howling void in our lives' (p.101).

This is a sketch of a complicated story about a gifted actress, whose mother played only a small part in her upbringing and whose father left when she was one year old. She relied on her nanny to be both mother and father to her, but Gertrude was not able to provide Massey with what might now be called today a 'secure' attachment. The result was that, as Massey wrote, 'I had never considered who I was. I relied on everyone else for their opinion. . . . I was like a raft on stormy seas, being blown in all directions . . . but I came home every night and there was Nanny' (p. 101). Massey's description of her relationship with her nanny raises an important point about delegated mothering and attachment. However loving and kind a nanny might be, she in fact can never be 'mother and father'. The nanny will always be a substitute for a mother, and as a result the child will have to manage maternal loss even if the nanny gives the child more love and attention than the mother.

If a loving and kind nanny does not necessarily provide a child with the internal armour to manage adult life, even though she may have provided some measure of security or stability, how much worse it is for a child who is imprisoned in the nursery with a cruel nanny. One of the most painful and most often quoted accounts of the hazards of handing one's child over to the care of another is to be found in the life of Lord Curzon (1859–1925). His emotional wellbeing was deformed by the treatment he received from Miss Paraman, though there is some discussion as to whether she was a nanny or a governess. (Gaythorne-Hardy, 1993; Hughes, 1993; Rose, 1969). She arrived when Curzon was five.

> She persecuted and beat us in the most cruel way and established over us a system of terrorism so complete that not one of us ever mustered up the courage to walk upstairs to tell our father or mother. . . . I suppose no children well-born and well placed ever cried so much or so justly.
>
> (Curzon quoted in Gaythorne-Hardy, 1993: pp. 302–3)

Her treatment of Lord Curzon rebounded upon his adult life in several ways. He became obsessed by his need to triumph over everyone in authority, even from his days at Eton. If one of his masters thought he was no good at a subject he would master it, on his own, and then to the surprise of the master he would win the prize for the subject. In later life, as Viceroy of India between 1898 and 1905 he found it impossible to delegate any authority to others or to have his authority challenged. It was said about him that 'the thought seems to arise in his mind . . . "I have given my opinion, I have even reiterated it in two or more dispatches, I am Viceroy of India, and confound you, how do you dare to set your opinion against mine"' (Rose, 1969: p. 359). By the end of his life, 'his *perpetual* desire for revenge' (Gaythorne-Hardy, 1993: p. 307) wore him out. He could only react with fury to any frustration either in his personal life or politically. He refused to have any contact with two of his three daughters when they dared to demand that they should be given their inheritance; their American mother had died in their early childhood and had left them a considerable fortune. Politically he found himself continually being cast aside at the moment when he had hoped he might be called to form a government. He died lonely and in great pain and ostracised from his second wife. 'It was her [Miss Paraman's] influence that in the end, after a glittering career, made him feel a failure and prevented him, ultimately, from being a happy man. It is enough for one woman to accomplish' (Gaythorne-Hardy, 1993: p. 308).

Less tragic but equally painful was the suffering that John Bowlby (1907–1990) experienced when his beloved nurse Minnie left him. Bowlby had had the typical experience of a privileged middle-class child. He spent his early childhood in a nursery wing of the family house and he only saw his parents for an hour in the evening (Holmes, 1993; Van Dijken, 1998). However when he was four his beloved nurse Minnie left. This was a trauma from which he never really recovered. Many years later and reflecting on this separation he wrote, 'For a child to be looked after entirely by a loving nanny and then for her to leave when he is two or three, or even four or five, can be almost as tragic as the loss of the mother' (Bowlby, 1958: p. 360). It is interesting that Bowlby is cautious in his description of the loss of 'a loving nanny'; he qualifies the heartbreak that her departure can occasion with the words that it is 'almost as tragic as the loss of a mother'. Has Bowlby added 'almost' because convention requires us to imagine that to be so? Or does the 'almost' hint at a paradoxical tragedy? A child who is looked after by a nanny will in the first instance suffer the loss of the mother when she hands her child over; but then if the nanny leaves before the child is ready to manage this next separation, the child suffers twice. This double loss can damage the child's confidence in the security of love and may leave the child with an inability to receive love open heartedly, as Groddeck (see Chapter 5) was aware. There lies the potential tragedy; Bowlby's 'almost' is a reminder that there was an original loss, the 'loss of the mother', which is then compounded if the nanny leaves too soon.

However it needs to be remembered that Bowlby's heartbreak at the loss of his beloved Minnie had a creative consequence. As a psychoanalyst he helped to change our angle of vision about the essential place the earliest caretaker has in the unfolding life of the child. He spelt out the damage that can be done if the infant suffers a premature separation from this central figure, and as a result much greater thought has been given to infant vulnerability and suffering. But in his emotional life, Holmes (1993) suggested, Bowlby was more comfortable to keep those he loved at a distance.

From these brief biographical accounts of the nanny she can be seen to be an influential figure in the internal lives of those she has looked after. Yet it seems that there is a continuing disregard of the significance of the nurse or nanny in psychological thinking. Does this suggest there may be other factors against accepting her significance? Like the wet nurse before her, does she disrupt or get in the way of the psychoanalytic belief in the central position of the biological mother? It is chilling to discover that the employment of the nanny may present the child with the same emotional conflict as we have seen in the previous chapters on wet nursing. A distance can be created between parents and their children if the nanny becomes the most important person in the child's life. One consequence of this shift in the emotional allegiance in the child, as we saw with Freud and Klein (see Chapter 5), is that mothers become idealised in the hope that this will heal or conceal the rupture that has already occurred. This is well described by Churchill, who had a wet nurse, a much loved nanny and a beautiful mother. He says about his mother that 'she shone for me like the Evening Star. . . . I loved her dearly – but at a distance.' His wet nurse is not remembered, except by extension when his wife commented, 'If it were left to him he'd have two nurses for the rest of his life' (Gaythorne-Hardy, 1993: p. 23). But about his nanny Everest with whom he kept contact all his life until she died when he was 20 he wrote, 'She had been my dearest and most intimate friend during the whole of the twenty years I had lived' (pp. 22–8).

The idealisation of the mother can lead to many difficulties, not least in the area of sexual identification. What are the emotional and sexual consequences of having an 'Evening Star' as the internalised image of one's mother on the one hand and a working-class nanny who is the 'dearest and most intimate friend' on the other? Gaythorne-Hardy (1993) throws out a challenging idea about the sexual development of the privileged Victorian and Edwardian male child who is brought up by a nanny. He wonders whether the sexual underworld of the Victorian era, where working-class girls entertained and comforted upper-class men, was the result of upper-class children being reared by working-class nannies. Were they 'acting out', as it were, the emotional split that had occurred as the result of having an idealised and distant mother and a working-class and comforting nanny? He cites a Victorian physician, William Acton (1813–1875) who believed that upper class women '(happily for them) are not much troubled with sexual feelings of any kind'. However men may have been led astray by 'Life among loose, or at least, low and vulgar women . . . to believe that she, and therefore all women, must have at least as strong passions as himself' (Gaythorne-Hardy, 1993: p. 93). In other words, lower-class women, such as nannies, can have sexual passions, whereas upper-class women, like mothers, are happily preserved from such animal spirits. William Acton was writing in the middle of the nineteenth century, and his treatise was called *The Functions and Disorders of the Reproductive Organs in Childhood, Youth, Adult Age and Advanced Life Considered in Physiological, Social and Moral Relations* (1857). It is not hard to imagine that Acton is writing from his own experience of having been brought up by a nanny and in some way his beliefs confirm the idea that a split does indeed take place in the mind of a child, emotionally and sexually, if it has 'two mothers'.

If boys may have conflictual sexual desires as a consequence of being brought up by a nanny, what about girls who are brought up by a nanny and who seldom see their mothers? Is their sexual identification equally compromised or confused? The aforementioned Mary Benson (1841–1918), the wife of E.H. Benson, all her life remained deeply attached to her nanny, Beth, and had difficulty in separating from her and in finding her sexual identity. Her mother, an extremely attractive woman, was widowed at the age of 32, leaving her with three sons and Mary, known as 'Minnie', a few months old. Minnie was a lively and intelligent girl who attracted her second cousin Edward Benson's attention when she was only eight. By the time she was 11 Edward had decided she was to be his future wife. Minnie's mother was told by Edward that 'if Minnie grew up the same sweet and clever girl that she was', he would like to make her his wife (Bolt, 2012: p. 6). Mrs Mary Segwick, Mary's mother, responded to Edward's proposal in an interesting way; she started to write to him and advise him not to mention his proposal even though he was constantly visiting the family. She then took to visiting him in Cambridge, where he was an undergraduate. After one such visit she wrote, 'I wish I could just come and take tea with you and stir your fire and stroke your face and have a nice chat with you this rainy windy evening.' Edward responded after another warm conversation they had had, 'I have had a day of you – would that it could have been more in thinking of you only. . . . How much I thought of you, and how much I wished for you, you may well fancy' (Bolt, 2012: p. 27).

Mrs Mary Sigwick was a woman of firm duty, even if we can glimpse a wobble when her sexual frustration and longing is aroused; and Edward Benson, as he began to embrace a life of discipline, scholarship and later the Church, was insistent that he would marry Minnie, not least to keep him out of sexual temptation. Mary Sigwick finally allowed Minnie to marry Edward when she was 18. But what did Minnie feel about this arrangement? She wrote a retrospective diary in 1876, 17 years after her marriage in 1859, and there are four significant entries: 'Ed. coming – *fear of him* – love? always a strain – never the love that 'casteth out fear'; 'Mother and Ed. both wanting my love – neither at all satisfied . . . misery . . . utter misery'; 'I had to satisfy Ed. by expressions of love and after was not true to Mama . . . I was influenced too strongly by him, without really loving him'; and finally, '*Go to Beth to comfort me*' (Bolt, 2012: p. 3. Italics added).

Minnie never found the love or sexual satisfaction that she hoped for with Edward, and after the birth of each of her six children her mental state became more and more fragile. However she had the comfort of Beth, her nanny, who took over the care of her children, as she spent increasing amounts of time at health spas, away from her children and Edward. Once she was away from her family ties she felt freer to follow her own desires, and her sexual desires were aroused by women. She was able to discover passion and fellowship with many women and the liberation for Minnie was that such passions were free from moral censure, for the sexual love between women was not recognised as adultery at the time. Several of her lovers joined the Benson household at different times and this allowed Mary and Edward to live more comfortably together.

It would be a mistake to attribute Minnie's love for women quite simply to her relationship with Beth but Minnie had never felt she could be herself with either her mother or Edward. It was only with her lovers and Beth that she felt she could be herself and imagine a life of her own. And here we come to the similarity with Massey's relationship with her beloved nanny. How satisfactory in terms of emotional development is the 'second mother', the nanny? Is there always something missing if she is internalised as the mother? Is that why psycho-analytic theory has ignored her for she represents neither mother nor father?

Are there other difficulties, as well, in taking on board the psychological effect of the nanny? Any nanny will communicate unconsciously her own inner world of fantasies and desires in bringing up another person's child. This constellation of feelings will in turn affect the internalised figure she becomes for the child. For instance, the nanny, and it needs to be remembered that she is unmarried, may bring her own anxieties about sexuality and reproduction. She may have turned away from the idea of giving birth with horror and echoed the sentiments of Queen Victoria who thought childbirth reduced one 'to being like a cow or a dog at such moments; when our poor nature becomes so very animal and unecstatic' (O'Connell, 2012). So the child may pick up the idea that sexuality is dangerous or destructive, or anyway to be avoided at all costs. What will that mean in terms of psychological development in the child? There may be a fantasy that nanny can remain with them forever; a figure who may never, psychologically, be given up or left or grown away from. This wish may be confirmed just because nanny is not married. Is that what happened to both Mary Benson and Anna Massey?

Alternatively nanny may bring a subtle and silent hostility towards the mother, so that the child unconsciously identifies with the nanny against the mother. 'Your mother is not fit to have children if she can't look after them' is the sort of attitude that many nannies in fact felt. The effect of this unspoken hostility may make the child anxious about mothering when it grows up. Mary Benson collapsed after the births of her children and had to hand them over to Beth. Did mothering make her too anxious? She was certainly experienced by her children as a wonderful playmate, who could invent games and roll and toss with them and some remarked on her child-like enthusiasm and vitality (Bolt, 2012). Many emotional configurations may add to the difficulty of integrating 'two mothers' in the child's mind. It is rare to find that a mother and nanny will lead a seamlessly harmonious life with each other or live in harmony in the inner world of the child.

Class and education add to these complicated strands. As we have seen the nanny will not have had the benefits of a secondary eduction, or as Massey poignantly wrote, 'Nanny of course . . . did not have the knowledge to assuage the deeper fears and neuroses that were developing in me' (Massey, 2006: p. 25). This in itself is not a barrier to being a good nanny but the child she is looking after may be torn between the belief systems of the nanny and the belief systems of the parents. Freud is a good case in point; his nurse took him to Catholic churches and told him about God, and these ideas will have been contrary to the Jewish beliefs of his family. The conflictual beliefs between Jews and Christians that he will have unconsciously picked up may have added to his later scepticism about religious faith.

So where does this exploration of the child-rearing practices of delegated motherhood lead? Has there been a fear of entering the area of 'second mothers' lest it is found that parents have not been as significant as psychological theories proposed? Has there been a wish to turn a blind eye towards parents who delegate the upbringing of their children to others? Has this led to an absence of thought about the impact of the nanny? To give an example, Hardin and Hardin (2004) drew attention to Peter Fonagy's clinical case in *The International Journal of Psychoanalysis* (2004) and Fonagy's absence of attention to the role the nanny and the housekeeper had in the case he presented of Miss A. Miss A was unable to make close relationships. She was the eldest of four girls and was brought up by a nanny and a housekeeper because her mother was an ambitious and professional 'courtroom advocate', who 'was hardly part of Miss A's early life at all' though she was Miss A's 'best friend' (Fonagy, 2004: p. 808). Fonagy tells us nothing more about the nanny and housekeeper, nor how long they stayed. Did Miss A have multiple caregivers? All we do learn is that Miss A ran away from home as a young girl and she remembers crying herself to sleep because her parents were not around when she was put to bed by her nanny. Nothing more. The difficulty that Fonagy encountered with Miss A was that,

> In the countertransference, I felt a certain shallowness after such a remark [how 'good' a particular session was], and I wondered what she was keeping at a safe distance by such idealisation. I also had an uncomfortable feeling of not knowing her as a person, as if our relationship was simultaneously a close and very distant one.
>
> (Fonagy, 2004: p. 808)

The question that needs to be asked is, was Miss A's difficulty in making close relationships related to the sudden disappearance of her nanny or housekeeper? We know she idealised her mother when she called her 'her best friend', which suggests there was a distant relationship between them. Did the nanny leave when she went to school? Or were there several nannies? If her mother was not around much in the early days of her life, as Fonagy indicates, it surely makes sense to imagine that her most significant attachment was to her nanny? Was the absence of the nanny, as reflected in the internal world of Miss A, a result of the difficulties that are encountered in the transference of those who have had a 'second mother'? (Hardin, 1985). Hardin, already mentioned in the previous chapter, makes an important point about the transference of those who have had multiple caregivers. 'Transferences of patients with a history of early primary surrogate mothering are often complicated, difficult to identify. Whatever their complexity, they reveal trauma of loss as a central issue in the developmental consequences of mothering' (Hardin, 1985: p. 627). The reason for this difficulty is that the early primary surrogate mothering involves a complex loss; in the first place the infant will have lost a close relationship with its own mother but then the child may lose the caretaker. One consequence is that the child may build up a 'life-long avoidance of further intimacy' (p. 627). Another major difficulty is that the two images of mother and nanny can become 'eclipsed' or 'merged' into one (p. 621). So what is needed is that the two images be prised apart and then the task of mourning the loss of the infant's relationship with its mother and the loss of the nanny can begin. Hardin believed that in many cases what needed to be refound was the devastating effect of the loss of love for the nanny. He also suggested that this re-finding was not helped by the idealised and distant relationship with the mother.

In Fonagy's relationship with his patient Miss A, his psychoanalytic interest focused upon Miss A's relationship with her father and in the transference with himself. Fonagy felt 'she is trying to make me submissive and useless, leaving me little to do except to agree with her' (Fonagy, 2004: p. 809). As the session nears the end, Fonagy addresses the distance between them in the following way, 'I think you are *very* frightened both of the damage and of the possibility of the change which could happen here, and that is perhaps why you feel you need to keep control'. As she leaves the session she replies, 'I feel frightened of you at the moment' (pp. 813–14).

Miss A's final remark is a heart-rending moment of fear; but the question is, is it the beginning of an awareness that Fonagy, like her mother, her nanny and housekeeper will leave her in the end? And this is where Hardin (1985) is particularily emphatic that patients, who have experienced the trauma of the loss of their early caretaker, need to become aware of the new loss that will have to be encountered in the therapeutic relationship, if they are to even begin to get to the foothills of their resistance to trusting anyone again. But Fonagy, for whatever reason in this session, ignores the possibility that Miss A may have 'a life-long avoidance of intimacy' that has been brought about by being brought up by nannies and housekeepers.

There follows upon Fonagy's clinical case two psychoanalytic commentaries and both seem to hint at a discomfort with the dynamics of the session that is described, though not put in the terms of Hardin. Dennis writes of a 'trap dynamic' that Fonagy and Miss A are in that has avoided 'her desire to love the analyst and to give him something that he would be glad to accept' (Dennis, 2004: p. 816). In other words, something is going on between Miss A and Fonagy that traps them both so that they are circling around each other. Has her love for her nanny been revived between them but both are unconscious of her presence? The other commentator, Hoffman, takes a slightly different angle but ends up in much the same position. He suggests Miss A has a 'wish to be cared for like a small child' while submitting in a masochistic way 'to be taken over by the analyst' (Hoffman, 2004: p. 819). Hoffman's discomfort seems to hint at a sado-masochistic entrapment; she longs to be looked after as a small child, and though Hoffman does not say it, this was the time when presumably she was being looked after by her nanny, but she fears that this revived love will bring about loss. Fonagy, however, feels she is trying to control him.

This clinical case brings to the fore the argument that we see in the psychoanalytic disregard for the surrogate mother and the effect she may have upon the emotional development of the child. The 'trap' that Miss A and Fonagy had fallen into was their mutual discounting of the nanny and housekeeper who were her principal caretakers in her early life. We have not been told about how long Miss A was in their care, but it makes psychological sense to suggest that her difficulty in effecting a close relationship with Fonagy reflects not only the distant and idealised relationship with her mother and Fonagy, but the lasting difficulty that her early delegated mothering had upon her. She felt safer if she avoided all close relationships. This distancing of herself from her analysis was compounded by Fonagy's failure to consider that there was a major loss that had been avoided in the transference. She longed to be in a mutually loving relationship but feared that it would involve submission to the unpredictable and traumatising loss of the other, Fonagy, the father, the mother but most importantly the surrogate mother, the nanny or nannies.

The nanny, like the wet nurse who preceded her, remains a shadowy presence in psychological theory, and it is hard not to conclude that her absence has been the result of the nineteenth- and twentieth-century idealisation of the nuclear family and the wish to ignore the fact that many parents have preferred to delegate their mothering to another.

Note

1. Perhaps one of the best known descriptions of the Nanny was by Belloc (1907):

    'And always keep a-hold of Nurse
    For fear of finding something worse.'

References

Belloc, H. (1907) [2012] *Cautionary Tales for Children*. London: Benediction Classics.

Bolt, R. (2012) *The Impossible Life of Mary Benson: The Extraordinary Life of Victorian Wife*. London: Atlantic Books.

Bowlby, J. (1958) *Can I Leave My Baby?* London: National Association for Mental Health.

Dennis, P. (2004) Commentary 1. *International Journal of Psychoanalysis* 85(4): 814–17.

Fonagy, P. (2004) Miss A. *International Journal of Psychoanalysis* 85(4): 807–14.

Fildes, V. (1986) *Breasts, Bottles and Babies.* Edinburgh: Edinburgh University Press.

Fildes, V. (1988) *Wet Nursing. A History from Antiquity to the Present.* Oxford: Basil Blackwell.

Gaythorne-Hardy, J. (1993) *The Rise and Fall of the British Nanny.* London: Weidenfeld & Nicolson.

Hardin, H.T. (1985) On the vicissitudes of early primary surrogate mothering. *Journal of American Psychoanalytic Association* 33: 609–29.

Hardin, H.T. and Hardin, D.T. (2004) On: Miss A. Letter. *International Journal of Psychoanalysis* 85(6): 1509–11.

Hoffman, I.Z. (2004) Commentary 2. *International Journal of Psychoanalysis* 85(4): 817–23.

Holmes, J. (1993) *John Bowlby and Attachment Theory.* London: Routledge.

Hughes, K. (1993) *The Victorian Governess.* London: The Hambledon Press.

Hunter, V. (1993) An interview with Hanna Segal. *Psychoanalytic Review* 80: 1–28.

Lubbock, S. (1939) *The Child in the Crystal.* London: Cape.

Massey, A. (2006) *Telling Some Tales.* London: Arrow Books.

Nead, L. (1990) *Myths of Sexuality: Representations of Women in Victorian Britain.* Oxford: Basil Blackwell.

O'Connell, J. (2012) Joy of slow communication. A most dreadful thing to witness. Blog. www.joyofslowcommunication.com/author/jockey76.

Proust, M. (1913) *Swann's Way*, C.K. Moncrieff (trans. 1922). Chatto & Windus; Penguin Books.

Rose, K. (1969) *Superior Person: A Portrait of Curzon and His Circle in Late Victorian England.* London: Camelot Press.

Streatfield, N. (2012). *Tea by the Nursery Fire: A Children's Nanny at the Turn of the Century.* London: Virago Press.

Turnball, R. (2011) *Shaftesbury: The Great Reformer.* Oxford: Lion Hudson.

Van Dijken, S. (1998) *John Bowlby: His Early Life.* London: Free Association Books.

Woolf, L. (1962) *Sowing.* London: Hogarth Press.

Young-Bruehl, E. (1989) *Anna Freud.* London: Macmillan.

Chapter 7

Trauma, attachment and melancholia

The central question that runs through this book is, what are the reasons for neglecting the wet nurse and the nanny in our psychological theories? She has held in her arms many figures in our cultural history, the most deprived as well as the most privileged, yet we seldom hear her name. This 'second mother' can leave painful 'impressions' upon the infant psyche when she leaves. She may have been the first love in a child's life and her loss may lead to permanent disruption in the infant mind. It is therefore necessary to explore some psychological theories on trauma, attachment and melancholia, in order to deepen our understanding of the lasting 'impression' the wet nurse and the nanny can leave and in so doing gain a better understanding of why her 'impression' has remained so hidden.

Until the early 1960s there was a widely accepted view that the infant was encased in its own narcissistic world and could not distinguish between the image of a caretaker or the image of its mother. For instance when Freud (1910c) was writing about Leonardo da Vinci and imagining Leonardo's early experience at his mother's breast, Freud seemed to imply that it was the experience of the nipple, not the person, which left the first impression of pleasure. He wrote, 'when we were still in our suckling days . . . and took our mother's (or wet nurse's) nipple in our mouth and sucked it', it was the feeding that was 'the first source of pleasure in life' (p. 87), not the experience of the relationship with the mother, or wet nurse, and her nipple; and such a view was endorsed later by Fenichel (1931). Fenichel challenged Groddeck's suggestion that an infant who had had a wet nurse had in its internal world 'two mothers'. On the contrary, he wrote, 'Clinical experience does not confirm this idea which seems highly improbable,' and the reason he gave was that 'in the beginning there are no images of objects' (pp. 87–8). The combination of these opinions of Freud and Fenichel led directly to the belief that in the infant mind the 'gestalt' of the nurse or nanny gets subsumed under the 'gestalt' of the mother and the difference between these two experiences is eroded (Mahler, 1961). This was a comforting idea, as was seen in the case history of Helene Deutsch's own son (see Chapter 5) who recovered, she believed, in nine days, from the loss of his surrogate mother. But at the same time as offering comfort to anxious mothers who might be wondering about the possible effect a nanny might be having on their precious child, such an idea altogether avoided confronting the anxiety that the child could be traumatised by the experience of having a wet nurse or nanny who left.

There has been a debate, which still continues, about the nature of trauma.[1] What do we mean when we say someone has been traumatised? Is a trauma triggered by an external event or is trauma the overwhelming of a psyche that cannot process the tumultuous feelings that have been aroused by the event? Freud in his early letters to Fliess believed that hysterical neuroses may have been caused by an infantile seduction by the father, that is to say, an external event. He soon repudiated such an idea for, as he wrote, 'such widespread perversions against children are not very probable' (Masson, 1985: p. 264). This then led him to suggest that this so-called perversion was in most cases a fantasy fuelled by an instinctual wish to be seduced by the father. So an uneasy balance was struck between 'real events' (Scott, 1996), 'constitutional factors' and psychic conflict aroused by unconscious wishes (Masson, 1985: p. 251). As Freud went more deeply into the causes of neuroses, and as he concentrated upon the way the inner world of fantasy is driven by instinctual wishes, external events were seen to be less important as the source of conflict. In the end Freud came to an uneasy balance between the causes of trauma; on the one hand there was war trauma as the result of 'external violence', but there was also trauma neuroses and these neuroses were caused by the fear or anxiety that the ego could be damaged by 'the enemy within' (Freud, 1919d: p. 210).[2]

One interesting way of bringing together Freud's two definitions of trauma was formulated by Krystal (1978). He suggested that there were two distinct types of trauma, infantile trauma and adult trauma. What makes his distinction so alive and memorable is that he was a Holocaust survivor, and so he brings to the debate a depth of meaning to the distinction between infantile and adult helplessness; only someone who had experienced the outer limit of adult trauma could manage to convey these subtle differences. Infantile trauma takes place, he believes, when the dependent infant is left in a state of unmitigated distress, such as being left to cry itself to sleep. If an infant is left to cry, in the end it will fall asleep. This falling asleep is not a peaceful place for the child, on the contrary, the child is 'in a state of total misery and exhaustion' (Krystal, 1978: p. 98). However for parents and caretakers and parenting gurus this state of sleep has served to reinforce the belief that it is all right to leave the child to cry for it will eventually calm down. What in fact is happening is that the infant is flooded with 'undifferentiated, somatic, preverbal, timeless, archaic affects' and 'this kind of experience is the most terrible and describable hell known to man, literally a fate worse than death' (p. 97). The result, if the infant is left in such an unbearable state continually and repeatedly, is that the infant will be left in an unending disregulated and frozen state and will be unwilling to engage again in a close relationship with another.[3]

In contrast to infantile trauma, in adult trauma the adult may fear that he or she is returning to an early infantile trauma, but Krystal believes 'it is not possible for an adult to have exactly the same kind of experience' (Krystal, 1978: p. 99). That is not to say that the traumas suffered in the death camps of the Holocaust were not unbearable, but, and this is the crucial point, the regression to a catatonic and zombie-like state, such as was the case with most of these victims, is not the complete regression that is experienced by the infant. The infant has not developed sufficiently to have any other recourse than to be overwhelmed and then it physiologically shuts down, whereas the adult does have recourse to defences, even if these lead to catatonia and surrender.

Krystal's description of infantile trauma has helped to refine our awareness of infant vulnerability, and this is still pertinent today as parenting gurus debate the best way to bring up a baby. There are still those who believe 'the child's will needs to be broken or it will rule the household'.[4] But does Krystal's distinction between infantile and adult trauma further the exploration of the traumatic effect that a 'second mother' may have upon the child she nurses? His contribution to an understanding of the infant mind came at a time when there had been a gradual shift in thinking about early infantile life and there was an increasing recognition of the significance of the earliest relationships in the formation of health and neuroses.[5] These new beliefs recognised the crucial importance of early biological attachment and at the same time the emphasis was being placed upon the developing infant mind in the arms, as it were, of the caretaker; in other words there was an increasing appreciation of the emotional development of the infant which first and foremost involved 'a two body relationship' of infant and mother (Winnicott, 1978: p. 99). But what takes place if the 'two body relationship' is not with the mother but with a wet nurse or a nanny with a bottle?

We now need to turn to attachment theory in order to try and answer that question. Here there is a theoretical position that helps to make sense of the traumatic effect that the 'two body relationship' between baby and caretaker may have if it is disrupted prematurely. John Bowlby (1958), who was the originator of the idea, rested his argument upon the ethological work of Konrad Lorenz (1935) on geese and their attachment to the first object that moves when they emerge from their shell. Bowlby suggested a similar biological need for attachment at the moment of birth if the human baby is to thrive psychologically. And as a result of Bowlby's work and that of other researchers, such as Ainsworth *et al.* (1978) and Main and Hesse (1990) on the subtle gradations of attachment, we now live in a different world, where it can be confidently asserted that an infant needs to be looked after by a consistent and enduring and well attuned caretaker if it is to manage the emotional complexities of life.

It has been said, both by critics and supporters, that Bowlby's attachment theory does not give a rich enough description of internal conflicts between love and hate or the role of sexuality or the subtle ways intelligence and imagination weave their imprint upon the psyche; although it needs to be remembered that Bowlby had a heart-felt understanding of the depression a child can feel when its beloved nanny leaves (see Chapter 4). In response to such criticism attachment theory has strengthened its claim by incorporating ideas from clinicians such as Fairbairn (1952) and Winnicott (1978) with their more detailed psychoanalytic theories of human development and conflict. What attachment theory needed was a theoretical understanding of the role of love. Both Freud (1915c) and Klein (1932) had based their psychoanalytic theory of infant development upon the idea that infant life was predicated on hate.[6]

It was clear that attachment theory faced in a different direction. How could an infant wish to become attached to someone they feared and hated? And to base infant development upon hatred certainly did not make biological sense. This is where Fairbairn's (1952) contribution is important. He disagreed with the idea that hate was the primary infant response to the maternal object. He believed hate was a response to deprivation of maternal care, or put another way, love was primary, and neurosis was a failure of love – 'the greatest need of a child is to obtain conclusive assurance (*a*) that he is genuinely loved as a person by his parents, and (*b*) that his parents genuinely accept his love'. Without this,

> Frustration of his desire to be loved as a person and to have his love accepted is the greatest trauma that a child can experience; and it is this trauma above all that creates fixation in the various forms of infantile sexuality to which a child is driven to resort in an attempt to compensate by substitutive satisfaction for the failure of his emotional relationships with his outer object.
>
> (Fairbairn, 1952: pp. 39–40)

And it is this view that underpins attachment theory today; infant trauma is associated with a lack of or the withdrawal of a loving relationship. But no understanding of attachment theory is complete without an appreciation of Winnicott (1978).

Winnicott has perhaps had the most profound impact upon the way we think about the newborn infant today. He, like Bowlby, observed mothers and babies and sensed the essential bonding that was necessary between mother and child if the child was to flourish. In one of his memorable remarks he said, *'There is no such thing as a baby* ... if you show me a baby you certainly show me also someone caring for the baby ... One sees a nursing couple'* (Winnicott, 1978: p. 99). It is this idea, that a newborn baby is in its early life part of a nursing couple, that not only enriches attachment theory and theories of the infant mind but supports the argument that if the nursing couple is a baby with a wet nurse or nanny, then we need to look at that experience to understand the unfurling of the emotional life of that infant.

Returning to the role of trauma; whether the trauma is described in terms of an infant being left in an unbearable state of distress, or whether the trauma is seen to occur from a lack of love or a lack of secure attachment, the consequences are conceived of in much the same way. The infant will retreat from contact with people and relationships and withdraw into its own self-comforting and over-sexualised world. One often repeated example is the infant with a depressed mother who cannot respond in a lively and communicative way to her child; in such a case the child does not have the means to manage its own bewildered feelings and as a result the infant retreats into a place where its emotional responses to life are impoverished.[7]

The accumulation of these ideas has added not only to the theoretical belief that we now live in an 'interpersonal world' but it has meant that the debate about the aetiology of trauma has shifted slightly. We no longer have to take sides between external and internal events and a more nuanced recognition is given to a dialogue that takes place between the internal predisposition of the infant, the external events that it encounters with its caretakers and, perhaps most importantly of all, the state of mind and the experiences that the caretaker brings to the encounter (Laplanche, 2009).[8] In the words of Russell (2006), 'It is an assault on truth to pretend that external reality does not exist. It is equally an assault on truth to pretend that *only* external reality exists' (p. 602).[9]

The widespread acceptance of the vulnerability of infants is to be seen in the work of many therapists.[10] The work of neurology and research into the development of the brain as well as the work in infant observation confirms this understanding.[11] They are all, from their different perspectives, acknowledging that the human psyche can only flourish in a two-person relationship. The primary need of an infant is to be held in a safe and empathic environment so that its brain and its emotional confidence can develop and if this containment is good enough then the infant will be able to manage better the inevitable conflicts that living a life involves.

One of the best accounts of this marrying up of psychoanalytic ideas on infant attachment and neurological research is in Gerhardt (2004) *Why Love Matters*. It is clear that she believes that it is 'particularly hazardous' to ignore a baby's cries, for it becomes stressed and produces 'high levels of cortisol . . . [that] can . . . affect the development of other neurotransmitter systems' which in turn upsets the biochemical systems of the developing brain and can 'make it more difficult for the individual to regulate himself in later life' (p. 65). This idea that the physiology of the brain and the response of the caretaker are interwoven adds another important texture to Krystal's theory of infantile trauma; the baby left too long in an unbearable state of distress is an infant who is deprived of love.

This complex interweaving of a two-person interactive perspective is also being supported by many scientists exploring the natural world today; this epistemology is captured by a neurologist and mathematician, Varela (1984), who wrote,

> Tradition would have it that experience is either subjective or an objective affair, that the world is there and we either see it as it is or we see it through our subjectivity. However . . . we may look at that quandary from a different perspective, that of participation and interpretation, where the subject and the object are inseparably enmeshed. This interdependence is revealed to the extent that nowhere can I start with a pure account of either.
>
> (quoted in Stern, 1985: p. 207)

It is an exciting moment to think that scientific epistemology is marrying up with interactive attachment theory. One result may be that the unresolved debate about whether psychoanalysis is a science can at last be laid to rest.[12]

The argument so far suggests that trauma theory and attachment theory have helped us to see more sensitively the vulnerability of the newborn infant. The recognition that psychic life begins in a two-person relationship allows us to imagine that if the wet nurse or a nanny has been the earliest caretaker, then she needs to be included in a psychoanalytic understanding of this early infant experience. The disavowal of her place within psychological theory, as we have seen, may well be due to a difficulty in recognising the trauma that accompanies her loss, if it is premature. Added to that there seems to have been a cultural prejudice against imagining that a woman of a lower class might have a signifi-cant influence upon the child she nurtures, especially if the nanny or wet nurse is black (see Chapter 4). There is however another more silent effect that she may leave upon the state of mind of the child she has nurtured. Segal (see Chapter 6) believed that the legacy of her multiple nannies had left her with 'a depressing streak, not anything damaging' (Hunter, 1993: p. 3). Such a view is being chal-lenged today by new evidence that suggests the loss of a caretaker or even multiple caretakers may leave the child with a more long-lasting melancholia.[13]

Fildes (1986) introduced the idea that many middle-class babies in the sixteenth and seventeenth centuries suffered from melancholia when they grew up. She suggested that Robert Burton's (1621) *Anatomy of Melancholy* became popular because it reflected a state of mind that was endemic to these middle-class wet-nursed babies. They had suffered a sudden weaning from their wet nurses when they got to the age of about two or three, such as we saw in the fictional case of Juliet in *Romeo and Juliet* where her Nurse put bitter aloes on her nipple (see Chapter 4). This sudden weaning was in most cases followed by the baby being returned home to its parents; so the baby, having already suffered one trauma by being taken away from its mother, suffered another trauma, the loss of the wet nurse and the familiar environment of the wet nurse. On this account, the child may have suffered from a proliferating state of melancholia.

What exactly is melancholia? And why would the loss of a wet nurse or nanny produce such a state of mind? The concept of melancholia comes from the late medieval idea of the four cardinal humours or fluids that are to be found in the human body and melancholia was seen as 'The condition of having too much "black bile"' (*Shorter Oxford English Dictionary*, 1973) with the result that the person became irascible and of gloomy spirits. When Freud (1917e) took up the idea of melancholia in *Mourning and Melancholia*, he described melancholia as 'a pathological disposition' (p. 243), which seemed to suggest he believed melancholia was constitutional, an idea that he never totally abandoned. But when he asked the question, why were melancholic people so self-denigrating, his answer was more complicated. Their melancholic thoughts were different from the thoughts of someone who was suddenly bereaved, for their melancholia persisted and seemed hard to give up. He described normal mourning as 'the reaction to the loss of a loved person, or to the loss of some abstraction which has taken the place of one, such as one's country, liberty, an ideal, and so on' (p. 243). And this state of mourning is gradually worked through as they accept that 'the loved object no longer exists' (p. 244). For the melancholic, things are different; the melancholic 'cannot see clearly what it is that has been lost, and it is all the more reasonable to suppose that the patient cannot consciously perceive what he has lost either' (p. 245). We are looking here at something more subtle than a dead body, as it were. The melancholic has lost some loved person and cannot recover or get over the loss, because as Freud says, 'The object-cathexis proved to have little power of resistance and was brought to an end' (p. 249). In other words, the loss occurred before there could be a conscious image of the lost person, or before there was a sufficient structure for mourning (Green, 1983). The beloved person has disappeared and yet, because she has never been mourned she has never been given up, instead she remains as a melancholic fixation in the internal world. 'Thus the shadow of the object fell upon the ego' (Freud, 1917e: p. 248). But 'the shadow of the object' falls upon the ego in a complicated way. The shadow is not entirely benign or without conflict for it is hated for its abandonment. The melancholic retreats into a cut off or frozen state, berating him or herself for the loss as well as being angry with the lost person for having gone.

Returning to the work of Hardin (1985, 1987, 1988a, b) and Hardin and Hardin (2000, 2004), they bring together these ideas of trauma, attachment and melancholia, and the problem of the loss of the wet nurse or nanny takes on new meaning. As we have seen, Hardin has championed the idea that psychoanalysis has ignored the effects that the loss of a surrogate mother can bring about. What is more significant is that his research over the last 20 years, with difficult or disconnected patients who are hard to reach, suggests that we may not have recognised that they may be unable to mourn the loss of an early surrogate mother, because nobody has 'seen' her. Therapists need to begin to ask whether there has been an early primary caretaker who left too soon. And the way of answering that question is through the experience within the transference. Hardin (1985) cites the clinical case of a man who had a surrogate mother for the first two years of his life. He came to see Hardin because he was having difficulty in managing a fantasy relationship with a woman at his work. He moved between feelings of calmness in her presence followed by periods of angry and aggressive fantasies towards her. His relationship with Hardin showed 'an intolerance of affection for me' (Hardin, 1985: p. 619). Hardin's understanding of both the transference and this man's fantasies about the woman at work, was that he was trying to retrieve memories of his experience with his surrogate mother, who left when he was two. In Mr C's experience she had been a loving and warm and soft presence (the woman at work about whom he had fantasies had the same name and black hair as his surrogate mother), but he had had to disavow his warm and tender feelings towards this 'Nan' and keep everyone, including Hardin, at a safe and hostile distance. One interesting fact that Hardin discovered was that as Mr C recovered memories of his lost and beloved 'Nan' she seemed to 'merge' into the image of his mother. Hardin explained this as a later defence or screen against the loss of his 'Nan', but he also is quite sure, in contradistinction to Fenichel or Mahler, that Mr C had 'more or less discrete images of the two mothers of his infancy' (Hardin, 1985: p. 621).

What is important about Hardin's work is that it gives a further explanation of why the surrogate mother has not been significant in the psychoanalytic literature. In many cases, as Freud was aware, she may not have been 'seen' or remembered consciously. But, with the major shift in psychoanalytic thinking towards a relational inter-subjective therapy, it becomes clearer that the hidden image of the surrogate mother may appear if the therapist is open to such an idea and is prepared to entertain the possibility that her ghostly presence still haunts the psyche of the child she nurtured.[14]

There has been an interesting development in ideas about surrogate mothering and melancholia in the US over the last 10 years that has been influenced by Hardin's work.[15] Questions have been asked about surrogate mothering; sometimes seen from the point of view of racial differences between infant and caretaker; sometimes from the angle of the immigrant having to adopt to a new culture. One striking question concerns the effect that the racial difference between a black nanny and a white child may have upon identity and loss, if the black nanny is socially denigrated.[16] The new emphasis on the relational and inter-subjective aspect of therapy brings to the forefront the idea that psychoanalysis is a search for meaning that takes place in the interaction between two people. For instance, Russell (2006) writes, 'the treatment relationship is a negotiation of what both patient and therapist *feel*. But the discovery of what one feels is also the discovery of who one is, and who one was. Feelings contain our perceptions, our memories and our losses.' This emphasis upon the idea that meaning is co-constructed has led to the idea that psychotherapy involves 'the re-finding, most especially, of lost relationships' (Russell, 2006: p. 620).

The significance of this viewpoint is that is has helped to open up lost and buried memories of unseen figures within the therapist as well as in the patient. These therapists no longer feel they must push back unwelcomed emotional stirrings within themselves, but are more confident that their disturbances may lead into further fruitful exploration in their work; and furthermore they claim that this pain or disquiet they are feeling is probably part of an interactive communication between therapist and patient. There is also a greater willingness to entertain the idea that enactments, either their own or their patients, may be a form of memory that had no words until it was discovered at the moment of enactment; in other words they embrace the idea that enactments are an inevitable part of the process of therapy. What is impressive about this way of imagining psychoanalysis is that it has begun to reveal, in both therapist and patient, accounts of lost and deeply hidden memories from early childhood and not least the world of the forgotten wet nurse, nanny or caretaker.

The work of Melanie Suchet (2004, 2007), a white South African therapist who was brought up in South Africa during the period of apartheid, is of particular significance as she reveals her own struggle to disinter her forgotten memories of her black nurse. She also brings a new political and social awareness to the role her nurse had played in her life. She had believed that she had left behind racial conflict when she left South Africa for the US until an African-American lesbian was referred to her for therapy. This woman, Sam, had been court-mandated to seek therapy rather than go to prison for her violence against her girlfriend. Suchet believed that the referrer had told Sam that she (Suchet) was a white expatriate South African, but for whatever reason, Sam seemed not to know. Under questioning Suchet told Sam that she had been brought up in South Africa; Sam was horrified and Suchet felt shamed. In the interstices of Suchet's heart she began to think about her own upbringing, in apartheid South Africa, and the struggle with what she called her own 'most hated self-states' (Suchet, 2004: p. 431), that is to say, her privileged position as a white child growing up in a racially oppressive regime. She faced again, in the consulting room, her position of power as a white therapist with a court-mandated African-American; this situation re-enacted the social positions of apartheid that were all too familiar to Suchet from her childhood. Sam left, Suchet believed, without either of them having resolved this power dynamic between them.

But Suchet continued to think about what it means to be white and she began to realise she needed to go back to her own early experience in South Africa. She had a black nanny, Dora. 'Dora, dark, chocolate brown Dora'. And there flooded back memories of Dora washing her and enfolding her in a large towel, Dora singing to her and kissing her, Dora feeding her 'miele pap' (Suchet, 2007: p. 872). She also remembered that Dora was allowed to invite her son, Abie, to visit two or three times a year and he and Suchet played together even though Abie was not allowed to swim in the swimming pool. And this memory faced Suchet with a sense of shame that the social structure required that Dora should give up the mothering of her own son in order to look after Suchet. Suchet agonisingly recalls, 'my happiness was at your expense' (Suchet, 2007: p. 874). Dora died when Suchet was 13 and disappeared suddenly one night, out of her life and un-mourned.

These memories are a powerful and moving testament to the love between Suchet and Dora, and Suchet brings to life a conflict that goes to the centre of a more extensive debate about shame and loss, and power and privilege, in the therapeutic encounter. The painful questions that Suchet asks herself are: 'I was your master, you were the slave'; but also 'you were my nanny-mommy. I was your child.' Finally she asks, 'I do not know who you were to me and who I was to you' (Suchet, 2007: p. 873). And it is with this sentence, 'I don't know who you were to me and who I was to you' that Suchet's work is chiefly concerned.

A black nanny raising a white child makes more transparent some of the social and sexual conflicts that have lain hidden in the muddy waters of white wet nurses and white nannies looking after white children. And the work of Suchet highlights issues of class, race and culture that confront any child brought up by a second or surrogate mother. However, what Suchet also brings to the debate is the indisputable fact that employing a black surrogate mother to look after a white child in a country such as South Africa or the US involves the dynamic of the master and the history of slavery. This view stretches into another uncomfortable idea; the idea that the dynamic is present in any case where one person holds economic power over an 'other', such as the fictional case of the Nurse in *Romeo and Juliet* (see Chapter 4). Suchet's work and the work of many others helps us to see more clearly the unconscious conflict that is created for any child who is handed over to another to be cared for. The parents become distanced from their child; the wet nurse/nanny/'slave' creates a bond with the child she nurtures; and finally in these patterns of child-rearing the looked after child experiences deep confusion about love and identity. In the memorable words of Suchet, 'I don't know who you were to me and who I was to you'.

The unconscious conflict that Suchet so eloquently describes gives rise, she suggests, to a state of melancholia in the looked after child. Freud, as already mentioned, believed melancholia was a form of pathological mourning, since the lost person is never given up and persists in unconscious memory as an ambivalent figure, with the traumatised child retreating into a narcissistic enclave of self-denigration. What is significant about the work of such therapists as Suchet, and others such as Eng and Han (2000) is that they accept that they are inhabited by feelings of melancholia, but what they challenge is the belief that this is pathological.

In the case of Suchet she is faced with a seemingly impossible psychic task of accepting that she suffers from melancholia and that part of this feeling has been brought about by her experience of having two mothers, one white and one black. How can she give up one of them and move on, as Freud's theory of mourning expects? 'I had a black and a white mother . . . How does one come to define a deep loving relationship that is socially devalued and ambiguous with the family. How does one reconcile such an intense intimate relationship with the status of servant?' (Suchet, 2007: p. 881). The task Suchet sets herself is to find a way of accepting her melancholia, not as pathological, but as an acceptance of the facts of the matter. At an unconscious level she identified with Dora, yet Dora, as a black person in apartheid South Africa, was 'a socially shamed other' (p. 880). In other words Suchet has to find a way of reconciling a 'shamed' social identity that she inhabits with Dora, as well as a 'shaming' social position as a white person.

Eng and Han (2000), who are Asian-Americans, have turned to another aspect of Freud's concept of melancholia, namely a melancholia that has its roots in 'environmental influences' (Freud, 1917e: p. 243). They delicately pick out the particular dilemma that is faced by those, in this case Asians, who move to a new country, the US, and hope to assimilate themselves into and be accepted by a different and dominant culture. They suggest that all such immigrants suffer from 'racial melancholia' (Eng and Han, 2000: p. 685). This melancholy can never be eradicated because they have lost their original home and culture and inter-generational traditions. They come to see that the ideal, which was embodied in the hope that a new country would provide them with new opportunities, can seldom be realised. They are outsiders or second-class citizens. A poignant case of 'racial melancholia' is illustrated by the case of a young Japanese child called Nelson. He came to the US when he was five, with his parents and siblings. His mother only spoke Japanese and was told by Nelson's kindergarten teacher that she should start to speak English to him. He mispronounced a word in class one day and his teacher rounded on him and asked him where he had learned to pronounce the word in this way. He replied that he had learned it from his mother. As Eng and Han comment, at that moment, 'Nelson could no longer mirror himself from his mother, in Japanese or in English'. And they go on to add,

> Although acquiring a new language (English) should be perceived as a positive cognitive development, what is not often acknowledged or emphasized enough is the concomitant psychic trauma triggered by the loss of what once had been safe, nurturing, and familiar to the young child (Japanese).
> (Eng and Han, 2000: p. 685)

Eng and Han then go on to call Nelson's suffering 'racial melancholia' because he feels himself to be a failure in the white community – he cannot pronounce English properly – but at the same time he can no longer feel quite safe with his mother tongue, Japanese. Later they comment, 'Nelson's Japanese identity becomes dissociated from him, repressed into the unconscious and transformed into a bad object'. And then they add significantly, 'Nelson's case history emphatically underscores the way in which good attachments to a primary object can be threatened and transformed into bad attachments *specifically through the axis of race*' (Eng and Han, 2000: pp. 688–9).

Eng and Han's account of 'racial melancholy' is another subtle way of describing Suchet's conflict as well. Her primary good nanny, Dora, became inflected by the racial and social conflict, '*the axis of race*', that was part of Suchet's white inheritance in South Africa. How could Suchet keep Dora as a good figure in her internal world while the social world, and presumably Suchet's parents as well, saw Dora as inferior? Suchet discovered that psychically she could not free herself from this conflict by leaving South Africa and embracing a liberal philosophy of racial equality in the US.

> The melancholia of the beneficiary, [the white person] . . . is the loss, a diminishment in the sense of self as we see through whiteness. It is the recognition that under the mantle of whiteness there is the perpetration of violence, terror, and the infliction of psychological damage.
> (Suchet, 2007: p. 873)

And she poignantly adds, 'We benefit ourselves, despite our beliefs, values, and ideals. Dora, when was it that I came to understand that my happiness was at your expense?' 'My happiness was at your expense' is perhaps the most telling phrase in all of Suchet's writing.

So to return to the question about the psychological consequences of having a wet nurse or nanny, it could be said that the psychological struggle that Suchet so movingly describes around her conflicted identification with her black nanny, Dora, and her simultaneous identification with the white culture of her family, gives a good reason why wet nurses and nannies have not been thought about as culturally important, either in the US or in Europe. What Suchet is helping us to see is that all children whose primary caretaker is of a different class or race will suffer from this melancholic conflict, such as in the cases of London, Smith and Oberndorf before her (see Chapter 4).

White middle-class children in Europe during the heyday of wet nursing surely had a conflict that had many similarities to the children brought up in societies where there was a clearer black and white social divide. Children who were 'farmed out' will have had to adapt to the class differences between the family of their wet nurse and the values of their family of origin. If we take the Nelson example from Eng and Han above, it does not stretch the imagination too far to believe that many children in Europe, being returned to their original families after a sojourn of several years in an agricultural and working-class environment, may have experienced the same melancholic dislocation. They may well have been mocked for their accent or manners and then have repressed the memory and disavowed the experience. Talleyrand gives no account in his *Memoirs* of his experience with his wet nurse except to say it encouraged him to face life with 'indifference'. It is not until someone like Suchet, who searches for forgotten aspects of herself in her earliest relationships, that we can begin to see why wet nurses and nannies may have been ignored. We have not had a way to reassemble the nurse's discrete position within the internal world of the child she has looked after because our social values have placed her as a second-class citizen, or 'slave', with no political power. This had led to the belief that she therefore had no emotional influence. It also needs to be added that it is only now that we can begin to appreciate the enormous emotional expense she has had to pay for the privilege of raising a child of the rich. There has been a careless disregard for her own family and, in the case of a wet nurse, or even Suchet's black nanny, for her own children. These children have suffered immeasurably from the absence of concern given to them by the privileged who have taken their mothers away.

The psychological ideas about attachment, trauma and melancholia that have been explored here have brought further understanding of the effects of surrogate mothering. The attachment to a 'second mother' may have traumatic consequences if it comes to a sudden end. If, on top of that, the caretaker remains unacknowledged and unmentioned, the child may well be left with deep and inarticulate feelings of melancholia. With the help of writers such as Hardin and Suchet, we can begin to see how important it is to recognise early infantile experiences with caretakers. What also needs to be recognised is that this surrogate mother, if she is full time, weakens the attachments that children make with their parents. We must begin to realise that although surrogate mothering may be necessary, in cases where the mother is not stable or dies, we should not be content in our therapeutic work to imagine that having a wet nurse or nanny does not leave its ineradicable imprint or 'impression'; 'Not anything damaging' (Segal, 1993) is not a good enough slogan to attach to the 'impression' that these caretakers may leave.

Notes

1. See Bohleber (2010); Garland (1998); Krystal (1978); Mucci (2013); Sandler *et al.* (1991).
2. We need to move beyond the debate as to whether psychoanalysis is only concerned with 'psychic reality' (Fonagy and Target, 1997: p. 216) and acknowledge that 'trauma and reality are necessarily linked together' (Mucci, 2013: p. 88). See also Alexander and Taylor, who suggest, 'The interplay between past and present is a core issue for all psychoanalytic thinkers' (2012: p. 7). Hopper adds an interesting philosophical insight that this schism between whether 'trauma really happened or was it imagined' reflects the intellectual debate about free will and determinism (2003: p. 208).
3. See Coles (2011); Fraiberg (1982); Gerhardt (2004); Schore (2002); Winnicott (1978).
4. Advice given to the author on the birth of her eldest son in 1959.
5. See Balint (1956); Bowlby (1958); Fairburn (1952); Fraiberg (1982); Ferenczi (1926); Spitz (1950); Suttie (1935); Trevarthen (2008); Winnicott (1978).
6. Freud (1915c) 'Hate as a relation to objects, is older than love' (p. 139). Klein (1932) 'hatred . . . [is] the basis for object relations . . . with . . . parents' (p. 135n).
7. For instance, Fraiberg (1982); Murray (1992); Trevarthen (2008).
8. Laplanche (2009) adds the idea that any encounter between a baby and its caretaker involves the unconscious of the caretaker. He calls this the *'primal seduction'* in which 'an adult proffers to a child verbal, non-verbal and even behavioural signifiers which are pregnant with unconscious sexual significations' (p. 126).
9. Such as Fonagy *et al.* (1991), Gerhardt (2004), Jones (2006), Main and Hesse (1990).
10. See Schore (2002) on neurology and Beebe and Lachman (2002), Murray (1992), Stern (1985), Trevarthen (2008) on infant observation.
11. Also Gerhardt (2004) suggests there is no such thing as a 'difficult infant', only a difficult parent or parents (p. 64).
12. See Bollas (1987: p. 6), but also Mucci (2013), Schore (2005), on the reality based aspects of trauma. Also Lear (2003) on subjectivity and objectivity.
13. In particular, Eng and Han (2000); Suchet (2007).
14. For example, Abraham and Torok (1994); Coles (2011); Davoine and Gaudilliere (2004).
15. Such writers as Altman (2004), Eng and Han (2000), Harris (2007), Hill (2008), Straker (2004), Suchet (2007) and White (2008).
16. In particular, Hill (2008) and Suchet, (2004, 2007), who have been influenced by the work of Ogden (2001), Russell (2006) and Stern (1985, 1998).

References

Abraham, N. and Torok, M. (1994) *The Shell and the Kernel*, N.T. Rand (ed. and trans.). Chicago: University of Chicago Press.

Ainsworth, M., Blehar, M., Waters, E. and Wall, S. (1978) *Patterns of Attachment: A Psychological Study of Strange Situation*. Hillsdale, N.J.: Lawrence Erlbaum Associates.

Alexander, S. and Taylor, B. (2012) *History and Psyche: Culture, Psychoanalysis, and the Past*. New York: Palgrave Macmillan.

Altman, N. (2004) History repeats itself in transference; countertransference. *Psychoanalytic Dialogues* 14: 807–14.

Balint, M. (1956) Problems of human pleasures. Classic essays in humanistic psychiatry. In: *International Psychoanalytic Library*. New York: Liveright.

Beebe, B. and Lachman, F. (2002) *Infant Research and Adult Treatment: Co-Constructing Interactions*. Hillsdale, N.J.: Analytic Press.

Bohleber, W. (2010) *Destructiveness, Intersubjectivity and Trauma*. London: Karnac.

Bollas, C. (1987) *The Shadow of the Object: Psychoanalysis of the Unthought Known*. New York: Columbia University Press.

Bowlby, J. (1958) *Can I Leave My Baby?* London: National Association for Mental Health.

Coles, P. (2011) *The Uninvited Guest from the Unremembered Past*. London: Karnac.

Davoine, F. and Gaudilliere, J.-M. (2004) *A History of Trauma: Whereof One Cannot Speak, Thereof One Cannot Stay Silent*. New York: Other Press.

Eng, D.L. and Han, S. (2000) A dialogue on racial melancholia. *Psychoanalytic Dialogue* 10: 667–700.

Fairbairn, W.R.D. (1952) *Psychoanalytic Studies of the Personality*. London: Routledge & Kegan Paul.

Fenichel, O. (1931) The pregenital antecedents of the Oedipus Complex. *International Journal of Psychoanalysis* 12: 141–66.

Ferenzi, S. (1926) *Further Contributions to the Theory and Technique of Psychoanalysis*. London: Maresfield Reprints.

Fildes, V. (1986) *Breasts, Bottles and Babies*. Edinburgh: Edinburgh University Press.

Fonagy, P., Steele, M., Moran, G., Steele, H. and Higitt, A. (1991) Measuring the ghost in the nursery: a survey of the main findings of the Anna Freud Centre/University College London parent-child study. *Bulletin of the Anna Freud Centre* 14: 115–31.

Fonagy, P. and Target, M. (1997) Perspectives on recovered memories. In: *Recovered Memories of Abuse. True or False*, J. Sandler and P. Fonagy (eds). London: Karnac Books.

Fraiberg, S. (1982) Pathological defenses in infancy. *Psychoanalytic Study of the Child* 51: 612–35.

Freud, S. (1910c) *Leonardo da Vinci and a Memory of His Childhood*. S.E.11. London: Hogarth Press.

Freud, S. (1915c) *Instincts and Their Vicissitudes*. S.E.14. London: Hogarth Press.

Freud, S. (1917e) *Mourning and Melancholia*. S.E.14. London: Hogarth Press.

Freud, S. (1919d) *Introduction to Psychoanalysis and War Neuroses*. S.E.17. London: Hogarth Press.

Garland, C. (ed.) (1988) *Understanding Trauma: A Psychoanalytical Approach*. London: Duckworth; Tavistock Clinic Series.

Gerhardt, S. (2004) *Why Love Matters: How Affection Shapes a Baby's Brain*. London: Routledge.

Green, A. (1983) The dead mother. In: *On Private Madness*. London: Rebus.

Hardin, H.T. (1985) On the vicissitudes of early primary surrogate mothering. *Journal of American Psychoanalytic Association* 33: 609–29.

Hardin, H.T. (1987) On the vicissitudes of Freud's early mothering – 1: Early environment and loss. *Psychoanalytic Quarterly* 56: 628–44.

Hardin, H.T. (1988a) On the vicissitudes of Freud's early mothering – 1i: Alienation from his biological mother. *Psychoanalytic Quarterly* 57: 72–86.

Hardin, H.T. (1988b) On the vicissitudes of Freud's early mothering – 1ii: Freiberg, Screen memory and loss. *Psychoanalytic Quarterly* 57: 209–23.

Hardin, H.T. and Hardin, D.H. (2000) On the vicissitudes of early primary surrogate mothering – II: Loss of the surrogate mother and arrest of mourning. *Journal of American Psychoanalytic Association* 48: 1229–58.

Hardin, H.T. and Hardin, D.T. (2004) On: Miss A. letter. *International Journal of Psychoanalysis* 85(6): 1509–11.

Harris, A. (2007) The house of difference: Enactment, a play in 3 scenes. In: *Relational Psychoanalysis. 3. New Voices*, M. Suchet, A. Harris and L. Aron (eds). *Psychoanalytic Dialogues* 18.

Hill, S. (2008) Reply to commentaries. *Psychoanalytic Dialogues* 18: 477–83.

Hopper, E. (2003) *The Social Unconscious. Selected Papers.* London; Philadelphia: Jessica Kingsley Publishers.

Hunter, V. (1993) An interview with Hanna Segal. *Psychoanalytic Review* 80: 1–28.

Jones, A. (2006) Levels of change in parent-infant psychotherapy. *Journal of Child Psychotherapy* 32(3): 295–311.

Klein, M. (1932) [1975] *The Psychoanalysis of Children.* New York: Delta Books.

Kyrstal, H. (1978) Trauma and affects. *Psychoanalytic Study of the Child* 33: 81–116.

Laplanche, J. (2009) Inzest und infantile Sexualität. *Psyche – Zeitschrift für Psychoanalyse* 63: 525–39.

Lear, J. (2003) *Therapeutic Action: An Earnest Plea for Irony.* London; New York: Karnac.

Lorenz, K. (1935) [1957] *Instructive Behaviour*, C.H. Schiller (ed.). New York: International University Press.

Mahler, M. (1961) Sadness and grief in childhood. *Psychoanalytic Study of the Child* 16: 332–51.

Main, M. and Hesse, E. (1990) Parents' unresolved traumatic experiences are related to infant disorganized attachment status: is frightened and/or frightening parental behavior the linking mechanism? In: *Attachment in the Preschool Years: Theory, Research and Intervention*, M.T. Greenberg, D. Chichetti and E. Cummings (eds). Chicago: University of Chicago Press.

Masson, J.M. (1985) *The Complete Letters of Sigmund Freud to Wilhelm Fliess, 1887–1904.* Cambridge, M.A.; London: Harvard University Press.

Mucci, C. (2013) *Beyond Individual and Collective Trauma: Intergenerational Transmission, Psychoanalytic Treatment, and the Dynamics of Forgiveness.* London: Karnac.

Murray, L. (1992) The impact of post-natal depression on infant development. *Journal of Child Psychology and Psychiatry* 33(3): 543–61.

Ogden, T.H. (2001) *Conversations at the Frontier of Dreaming.* London; New York: Karnac.

Russell, P.L. (2006) Trauma, repetition, and affect. *Contemporary Psychoanalysis* 42: 601–20.

Sandler, J., Dreher, A.D. and Drews, S. (1991) An approach to conceptual research in psychoanalysis illustrated by a consideration of psychic trauma. *International Review of Psychoanalysis* 18(2): 169–200.

Schore, A.N. (2002) Advances in neuropsychoanalysis, attachment theory, and trauma research: implications for self psychology. *Psychoanalytic Inquiry* 22: 433–84.

Schore, A.N. (2005) Attachment, affect regulation, and the developing right brain: linking developmental neuroscience to pediatrics. *Pediatrics in Review* 26: 204–17.

Scott, A. (1996) *Real Events Revisited: Fantasy, Memory and Psychoanalysis.* London: Virago.

Segal, H. (1993) An interview with Hanna Segal. In: Hunter, V. (1993). *Psychoanalytic Review* 80: 1–28.

Shorter Oxford English Dictionary (1973) Oxford: Oxford University Press.

Spitz, R.A. (1950) Anxiety in infancy: a study in its manifestations in the first year of life. *International Journal of Psychoanalysis* 31: 131–43.

Stern, D.N. (1985) *The Interpersonal World of the Child: A View from Psychoanalysis and Developmental Psychology.* New York: Basic Books.

Stern, D.N., Sander, L.W., Nahum, J.P., Harrison, A.M., Lyons-Ruth, K., Morgan, A.C., Bruschweiler-Stern, N. and Tronick, E.Z. (1998) Non-interpretive mechanisms in psychoanalytic psychotherapy: the 'something more' than interpretation. *International Journal of Psychoanalysis* 79: 903–21.

Straker, G. (2004) Race for cover: castrated whiteness, perverse consequences. *Psychoanalytic Dialogues* 14: 405–22.

Suchet, M. (2004) A relational encounter with race. *Psychoanalytic Dialogues* 14: 423–38.

Suchet, M. (2007) Unravelling whiteness. *Psychoanalytic Dialogues* 17: 667–886.

Suttie, I.D. (1935) [1988] *The Origins of Love and Hate.* London: Free Association Books.

Trevarthen, C. (2008) Thought in motion: interdisciplinary approaches to mind and body. Lecture at Tavistock Centre. 5–6 September. New York: Analytic Press.

White, C. (2008) Crossing boundaries: commentary on paper by Sarah Hill. *Psychoanalytic Dialogues* 18: 466–76.

Winnicott, D.W. (1978) *Through Pediatrics to Psychoanalysis.* London: Hogarth Press.

Chapter 8

Natural bonds

Suchet (2004, 2007) and others suggest that an inter-subjective model of the mind opens up the possibility, within therapy, of 'the re-finding . . . of lost relationships' (Russell, 2006: p. 206). This was after all Freud's concern when he searched for the 'impression' of his nurse. Suchet (2007) in particular, suggested that the re-finding of lost relationships is made possible through the dialectical relationship between therapist and patient. She realised that she had failed to recognise the importance of her relationship with her black nurse because of her own hidden racial prejudices that were endemic in the South African society in which she had been brought up. This failure to recognise the complicated internal models she had of two mothers, one black and one white, impeded the therapy she was engaged in with a black American patient. The recognition that therapists may need to discover their own disavowed and lost relationships, while working with a patient, subtly twists the axis of therapy. Theoretically what underpins the model of the inter-subjective relationship is the idea that some memories can only be discovered through enactments within the present relationship, as both therapist and patient struggle to understand and give meaning to the 'non-verbal contents of the patient's communication' (Grinberg, 1997: p. 12).

The reason that some lost relationships can only be re-found through enactments within therapy can be explained by recent theories about memory. There is a new body of evidence suggesting that the earliest experiences of childhood are not recorded in an unconscious memory that can be recovered from the repressed unconscious, as suggested by Freud (1926d). On the contrary, some clinicians propose that 'there are a number of kinds of memory' (Pally, 1997: p. 1223).[1] One of these 'kinds of memory' is declarative or explicit memory in which conscious recollection of experiences can be recalled. Even in cases where past history has been consciously forgotten, it is still possible for these memories to be recovered. In contrast to these potentially recoverable memories there is a non-declarative or implicit memory, which 'will not translate directly into explicit memories' (Weiskrantz, 1997: p. 20–1). One example, often given, of this implicit or non-declarative memory, is the way learning to ride a bicycle is laid down. We do not have to relearn or recall how it is done each time we ride a bicycle, it is outside our awareness but, and this is the crucial point, the knowledge is not repressed, it is merely 'non-conscious' (Clyman, 1991: p. 352). There is, however, an area of memory that is more complex than this implicit memory, such as learning how to ride a bicycle. There is an implicit memory that is laid down in early life that is internalised as a model of relating. Such memories are associated with Bowlby's (1973) idea that the child will form an attachment to the caregiver and his or her way of handling the child. This implicit memory has its foundation in 'implicit relational knowing'; that is to say, the infant learns 'how to be with others' (Stern et al., 1998: pp. 903–5) and this learning will not form a part of a repressed unconscious that can be discovered or accessed in therapy by the 'talking cure'. It will be known through the way patient and therapist relate to each other. Schore (2002) suggests that if trauma has been suffered in the first two or three years of life, and he is referring to the trauma of the failure of consistent and well regulated attachment, then therapy may become a 'communicating cure' (p. 472), in which the early steps of being with another have to be re-learned.

What is interesting about this last idea, about an 'implicit relational knowing' (Stern et al., 1998: pp. 903–5), is that a new way of thinking about the forgotten wet nurse or nanny emerges. The memories of a child who has been 'farmed out' for the first two or three years of its life, or has been looked after almost entirely by a nanny, may have memories of these early caretakers that will largely lie in implicit relational memory and not a memory that will 'translate directly into explicit memories' (Weiskrantz, 1997: pp. 20–1). Such children will be left with unconscious memories of ways of being with the other, which will be part of their internalised life, but, as with Freud, there may be no more than a vague 'impression' of her smell or of the subtle way she physically communicated and held the child. This new research is important when considering wet nurses and nannies as it helps to add another layer of understanding as to why these figures have been so absent from psychoanalytic interest. They may have lain in implicit relational memory, without the words to recall them.

But that is not all that is significant about 'implicit relational knowing'. Suchet et al. (see Chapter 7) make explicit the way the relational memory of children nursed by someone of a different race has been extraordinarily difficult to confront, not least because of racial prejudice. In South Africa and the Southern states of America, for instance, a white child and its black wet nurse or nanny will be part of a history that involves not only racial difference but a history of slavery. These factors are part of an important cultural legacy that must not be forgotten. However what has also impeded this 'relational knowing' is that an economic system has underpinned all domestic relationships with wet nurses and nannies and has imposed a silent constraint that seeks to deny the undertow of power, race and class that sustains such caretaking relationships.[2]

The economic transaction of employing a wet nurse or nanny is common to all accounts. And even to this day the financial contract between wet nurse or nanny and employer is believed to be a satisfactory arrangement for all concerned, as Shorter (1977) (see Chapter 1) pointed out. But what this satisfactory economic arrangement has obscured is the underlying de-humanising effect that it can have upon all those concerned in the transaction. In *What Money Can't Buy* (2012), Michael Sandel raises an uncomfortable question about money that is pertinent to the employment of the wet nurse and the nanny. He develops the idea that there is an erosion of natural human concerns when it is believed that money can buy anything. 'Market incentives erode or crowd out non-market incentives' by denying that 'markets . . . embody certain norms'. But in fact, Sandel maintains, markets 'presuppose – and promote – certain ways of valuing the goods being exchanged' (Sandel, 2012: p. 64). He takes as an example a study of child-care centres in Israel. Many parents would turn up late to pick up their child at the end of the day and this meant that a teacher had to stay until the parents arrived. So it was decided that a system of fines should be introduced in the hope that parents might be persuaded to pick up their children on time. In fact the reverse happened and parents continued to arrive late; but now instead of feeling guilty at arriving late they believed they were buying into this service, and the norm, of picking up your child on time, was eroded. Money could buy them out of their difficulty, or one might add, responsibility.

We can see a similar erosion of norms about human and infant welfare when considering wet nursing from the point of view of the buying and selling of 'mother's milk'. Fildes (1988) pointed out that 'Wet nursing, like prostitution, was one of two available sources of income for poor young women. They could at all times earn their keep by becoming pregnant and selling their milk' (p. 246). And in putting together these two female activities, wet nursing and prostitution, Fildes draws attention to the financial transaction that accompanies both these activities. They involve the commercialisation of the female body; it can be bought and its products can be sold.[3] The fact that women could sell their milk was of course welcomed by those who needed the money, and in the cases where an infant was orphaned at birth, such a transaction meant that the child was provided with a means of survival. But whether buying in 'mother's milk', or a nanny with a bottle, or selling one's services, there has been a subtle erosion of human concern about the meaning of this transaction.

In 1887 Freud employed a Moravian wet nurse for his eldest daughter, Mathilde. He wrote to his mother-in-law and his sister-in-law, 'The story of the wet nurse is as follows, she produced less and less milk; at the time she devoured outrageous quantities of everything imaginable; finally she got indigestion, felt miserable, and on top of it all the child developed a *green* stool' (Freud, 1961: p. 235). She was dismissed and a second wet nurse arrived who was more satisfactory and 'on whom the child has already fastened itself' (p. 235). Freud's final comment about the first wet nurse was 'the first one is going home this evening, enriched by beautiful memories' (p. 235).

There are several things that can be said about that brief excerpt. The tone of the 'beautiful memories' he imagined the wet nurse might have had places her squarely in the role of the discounted and derided servant. Moreover, by employing the wet nurse himself, Freud seemed to be following in a long paternalistic tradition, that was at its height in Renaissance Florence, in which it was always the father who negotiated the contract between the family of the wet nurse and the money she would be paid. In such circumstances, as Klapisch-Zuber (1987) has argued, the mother 'cuts an uncertain figure' while 'What is exchanged – here – money, child, milk – seems out of her grasp' (p. 159). There is no evidence that Freud's wife Martha was an 'uncertain figure' in the Freud household (Behling, 2005).[4] However, the fact that it was men who dealt with the financial transactions of employing a wet nurse encouraged the disruption of the delicate threads that surround a mother and baby, especially if the mother was presumed to have no say in the matter. The fact that it was men who negotiated this transaction contributed to the belief that wet nursing was merely a financial contract.

There is another point that needs to be considered regarding Freud's anxiety about this first wet nurse; he seemed horrified that Mathilde produced a '*green stool*' and he attributed this to the wet nurse's gastronomic habits. We have seen throughout this book that the condition of the milk of the wet nurse was of prime consideration when she was first employed. Furthermore it was believed that if she became pregnant while feeding her nursling, the nursling would be poisoned. Freud seems to be reflecting similar anxieties in which Mathilde was being harmed by the milk of the wet nurse due to the nurse's eating habits. But what is the reason for this anxiety? Klapisch-Zuber (1987) makes an interesting suggestion: 'Behind the violence of the . . . reaction, should we not read . . . at least ambiguous sentiments and feelings of guilt?' (p. 160). Klapisch-Zuber's observation highlights a conflict that has always underpinned the employment of wet nurses. The financial transaction of buying in 'mother's milk' has led to the disregard of the emotional consequences of such a contract, yet the dread that the milk of the wet nurse might be poisoning the child reflects feelings of guilt that have been projected on to her.

Neither Freud nor Klein expressed conscious feelings of guilt about employing wet nurses for their children and furthermore they seem to have been unconcerned about the psychological effect that wet nursing might be having upon their children. Mathilde, apparently, was not affected by the change of wet nurse and there was no expression of concern or interest about the welfare of the wet nurse's child. So Sandel's argument, that money can blind the buyers to the moral consequences of financial transactions, is borne out by the actions of both Freud and Klein. They could buy into the service and this diminished their capacity to think about the emotional ramifications of this child-care practice.[5] In their defence it could be said that it was a socially acceptable way of providing milk for one's child; but nevertheless their absence of psychological thoughtfulness about the emotional complexity of the transaction is puzzling, especially in the light of their deep compassion for human suffering, which was the hallmark of their psychoanalytic thinking.

The idea that guilt feelings can be aroused by the buying in of child-care, helps to explain the lack of sensitivity and thoughtfulness there has been towards the child of the wet nurse. There was a supposition that the wet nurse could make proper provision for her child once her services had been bought. So, in Florence during the Renaissance, it is found that 'Florentines were insensitive to the moral handicap that weighed on their nurses – women who had to give up their own children' (Klapisch-Zuber, 1987: p. 140) and this sentiment seems to have been echoed throughout Europe. In George Moore's (1894) novel, *Esther Waters*, Mrs Rivers, on employing Esther as a wet nurse, told her to make proper provision for her own baby as she did not want Esther's baby to die, as had the children of two previous wet nurses she had employed. The implication of this remark was that Mrs Rivers was irritated by the death of these babies as it had intruded upon her life; furthermore she was communicating that she was not to be bothered about how Esther was to provide for her own baby. It was not until the middle of the nineteenth century when several scandals about 'baby farming' forced the plight of these discarded babies onto the conscience of society (see Chapter 2) that the general public awoke to the realisation that employing a wet nurse often meant the death of the wet nurse's own child.

There is a further point that can be made about the commercialisation of 'mother's milk'; wet nursing involved the buying in of human care. The wet nurse was entrusted with far more than supplying milk to her nursling. The child was expected not just to survive but also to flourish and it often did. But, can love, which all children need, be provided in this commercial way? Or, to put it another way, 'Is love a "resource"' (Hochschild, 2003: p. 22) which can be bought? It has already been suggested that the buying and selling of 'mother's milk' led to an erosion of human concerns about the wet nurse and her own child. But the buying in of 'mother's milk' also diminished the value of maternal care; not only could 'mother's milk' be bought, but so could mother's love.

This idea has been vividly portrayed by Hochschild (2003) writing about the present popularity, in the US and the UK, of buying in child-care from the impoverished countries of the 'Third World'. Busy mothers and fathers, in the 'First World', cannot afford to look after their own children and keep their jobs, so they buy in child-care from mothers from impoverished areas like the Philippines. Here there are many mothers who are desperate for money to provide for their own children and to give them a better life, so they come to the West, leaving their own children behind, and look after the babies of the rich. This creates a 'hidden and wrenching trend' for these mothers, who become embroiled in a 'care drain'. They love and take care of another's child, and, as with the wet nurse, this work provides them with money to send back to their own children. But the hidden side to this financial transaction is that the nurse gives her love to someone else's child while depriving her own child of the love it needs. It is difficult not to agree with Hochschild, who describes this form of child-care as 'a global heart transplant' (p. 22); a 'heart transplant' in which many hearts get broken. But what is also chilling about this modern method of child-care is that it has many echoes from the past. 'Third World' children are deprived of their mother, as were the children of wet nurses; 'First World' children are deprived of their mother, as were the children who were 'farmed out' to wet nurses; and the one thing that keeps the whole system going is money and the unspoken belief that love is a resource that can be bought. Here one sees a repetition of the erosion of human thoughtfulness in all those who are involved in the commercial transaction of buying and selling child-care. It seems clear that the belief that money can buy anything not only provides an explanation for the de-humanising of the wet nurse or nanny but also contributes to an understanding of why she seldom appears in the pages of our social history. She has been seen as no more than a business commodity.

There is, however, another point that needs to be made about the nurse that puts her into the heart of a continuing debate about the best way to bring up a child. In many manuals on the proper way to bring up a child, even to this day, there seems to have been two distinct responses to the birth of a baby. There has been a 'child-centred' approach to infancy, in which the inner life of children can be imagined without too much fear or anxiety and the role of empathy plays an important part in the child's upbringing. In contrast there has been an 'adult-centred' view about children that is more apprehensive and anxious. The nature of the child is believed to be problematic and this gives rise to questions about the child's will and whether it needs to be curbed or broken. In such cases, strict rules are often laid down that can lead to harsh discipline and cruelty.[6]

The child-centred approach is exemplified by Aulus Gellius (120–180 AD), already mentioned in Chapter 1. Gellius wrote of the earliest relationship of the infant to the breast in a way that seems to be familiar to attachment theory, 'the natural affection of a child, its fondness, its familiarity, is directed to that object only from which it receives its nourishment' (Gellius, 2012: p. 326). What was also psychologically astute was his observation that, if the child has a wet nurse, the child will become emotionally distanced from the mother and the mother will fail to bond with her child because you 'destroy the foundations of natural affection'. He then goes on to say, 'children thus brought up may seem to love their father or mother, [but] that regard is in great measure not natural, but the result of civil obligation and opinion' (pp. 326–7). Not only is the bond between mother and child broken, but the child will grow up with a false sense of love and will only be mouthing obligations and opinions. Surely this is one of the earliest psychological accounts of the 'false self' (Winnicott, 1978)? A final and important insight that Gellius brings to his child-centred approach to infancy is the way the method of wet nursing gets handed down across the generations, in spite of the evidence that it breaks the bonds of natural affection between parents and child. He cites the example of a young mother, who would have had the natural inclination to feed her own baby, but her mother persuades her that she needs to rest and that if she employed a wet nurse she would recover more quickly from the birth. The mother adds that 'suckling an infant' is a 'toilsome and difficult task' and this reinforces her argument that her daughter should employ a wet nurse (Gellius, 2012: p. 322). In this way the mother hands on a tradition of wet nursing to her daughter in spite of the fact that it cuts across the grain of natural inclination.

Another 'child-centred' approach to child-care was raised by St Anselm (1033–1109). He argued against the social belief that children needed to be harshly disciplined. He was concerned in particular with those children who had suffered the cruel procedure of 'oblation'; that is to say, they had been given up, at a young age, as an offering to a monastic order (see Chapter 2, note 2). He was disturbed by the harsh treatment that these children suffered and likened child rearing to planting a tree. If you do not treat children with kindness they will have 'no faith in your goodness but believe that all your actions proceed from hatred and malice against them' (quoted in Cunningham, 2006: p. 29). His belief in the need to treat children with kindness, it is said, stemmed from his own experience of a concerned mother. He had persuaded his parents to send him to school when he was about seven. He was so rigorously treated by his teacher that he was 'almost driven out of his mind'. He was returned home, unable to speak, as he was so filled with anxiety. His mother was deeply troubled by his state of mind and ordered all the servants to allow him complete freedom to do whatever he wanted and said that he was not to be crossed in any way. He soon recovered his capacity to communicate, and was forever grateful to his sensitive mother and had great compassion for children (see McLaughlin, 1976: p. 127).

Sir Thomas More (1478–1535) is another example, on all accounts, of someone who was an outstanding father to his children (Ackroyd, 1999).[7] His loving concern is exemplified in a letter he wrote to his three daughters.

> It is not so strange that I love you with my whole heart, for being a father is not a tie to be ignored. Nature in her wisdom has attached the parent to the child and bound them spiritually together with a Herculean knot. You know, for example, how often I kissed you, how seldom I whipped you. My whip was invariably a *peacock's tail*.
>
> (Tucker, 1974: p. 248)

Finally, Mary Carpenter (1807–1877), an early social reformer, who spent her life concerned with the children of 'the perishing and dangerous classes', wrote of her belief that 'Love must be the ruling sentiment of all who attempt to influence and guide children. . . . it is an absolute necessity of their nature, and when it is denied them, they become no longer children' (Manton, 1976: p. 121). All these writers seem unafraid of children and furthermore, in their different ways, asserted their belief that loving care was essential if children were to flourish.

Yet in spite of these beliefs and cogent arguments that had been expressed for 2000 years many parents continued in other habits and customs with which they were familiar and preferred to ignore Gellius' insights about early attachment and affection. In Gellius' example of the mother who believed that breast feeding was 'a toilsome and difficult task' she was reflecting the opposite of a 'child-centred view' of children, namely, an 'adult-centred view' that children were a burden and were best cared for by others. There are other treatises on child-rearing that express similar beliefs about children and at the most extreme end of this spectrum parents are encouraged to break their children's wills for they are 'wanton and foolish . . . [and need] to be broken by education and correction' (Fletcher, 2008:

p. 3). Consider this sixteenth-century account of the way the parents of Lady Jane Grey (1536–1554) treated her:

> One of the greatest benefits that God ever gave me is that he sent me so sharp and severe parents. . . . For when I am in the presence either of father or mother, whether I speak, keep silence, sit, stand, or go, or eat, drink, be merry or sad, be sewing, playing, dancing, or doing any thing else, I must do it, as it were, in such weight, measure and number, even so perfectly as God made the world, else I am so sharply taunted, so cruelly threatened, yes, presently sometimes with pinches, nippes, and bobs, and some ways which I will not name for the honour I bear them, so without measure misordered, that I think myself in hell.
>
> (Tucker, 1974: p. 248)

This view of the proper way to bring up a child reflects an anxious concern, not only about an appropriate Christian education, but also a fear of the child's power. Grey's parents seemed to believe that the best way to instil Christian virtue was through the savage onslaught of a whip, a taunt or a pinch.[8]

This 'adult-centred' view of children continues to this day and is well described in Elizabeth Young-Bruehl's (2012) recent book, *Childism: Confronting Prejudice Against Children*. She suggests that there has been a deep fear about children that has run throughout most societies. In the US there is a belief 'that children are dangerous and burdensome to society, and that childhood is a time when discipline is the paramount parent responsibility' (p. 3). This fear is reflected in an 'anti-child culture' (p. 6) in which more children are incarcerated than anywhere else in the world. There are currently half a million children between the ages of 11 and 17 languishing in US prisons, many of whom are victims of abuse and neglect. This is not the place to enter into a debate about this particular US 'anti-child culture'; but what is of interest is that Young-Bruehl seems to confirm the view that childhood can arouse deep anxieties in adults that can lead them to deal harshly with their children.

Where does the nurse come into this debate? The nurse, as caretaker of the infant child, has been part of the conflicting ideas that have beset the upbringing of the young. In some cases she must have been expected to break the will of the child, whereas in other cases, she might have proffered her breast on demand, as in the case of Melanie Klein's wet nurse (see Chapter 5). The views of the parents, that she will have been expected to endorse, have put her into an ambiguous position. In Chapter 6 it was suggested that there were many instances of nannies wondering why parents bothered to have children as they took such little interest in them. This view seems to endorse the idea that some parents were despised, or at least the nannies felt superior. From the point of view of the parents, delegating the care of their children to others may have rescued them from confronting painful emotions aroused by the dependency and vulnerability of their children, but they may nevertheless have felt guilt and shame at their inadequacy. The wet nurse or nanny will have been a witness to the parents' fear of treating their child with the love it needs, if it is to flourish; she will have seen the parents defending themselves against their anxiety, perhaps by courting an indifference to their child. Whatever the emotions the parents bring to parenthood, the delegated mother is both observer and container of parental feelings and this inevitably puts her in a powerful position.

However, as we have seen, there has been a tendency to despise her and deny that she has ever held a position of significance in a child's life, and in this way, the ambivalent emotions the parents may have had towards their child get projected onto her. In cases where the child was failing to thrive, she was believed to be poisoning the child; in other cases she was seen as inadequate, or vulgar, and sometimes called 'an ogress' (Fildes, 1988).[9] In contrast to this projected image of the delegated mother as ogress or poisoner or merely vulgar, she may have offered the only beacon of love in the disordered life of a child whose parents looked upon it with anxiety and fear. In such cases she can be hated for her maternal capacity. It is because the nurse has been a witness to the many and complicated emotions parents can have towards their children that we find yet another reason for putting her out of sight. It is not hard to imagine that part of the silence that has been imposed upon her may be echoing with the shame that parents have felt as they put their child in her arms.

On the cover of this book there is a charcoal drawing by Leonardo da Vinci (1452–1519) of the Virgin holding the Christ Child on her knee. She is sitting between the knees of her mother Saint Anne, and Saint John the Baptist leans into the picture draped across one knee of Saint Anne. A striking feature of this drawing is that Saint Anne looks the same age as her daughter Mary. In Freud's (1910c) essay on Leonardo he reminds us, that though there is little recorded history of Leonardo's early life, he had two mothers. He was the illegitimate child of Ser Piero da Vinci and his mother, Caterina, was probably a peasant girl. It is not known how long Leonardo remained with his mother; Freud suggests he was between three and five when he left her; but what is certain is that as a young child he was taken into his father's household and he was brought up by his step-mother, who was good to him. There are no records to suggest he saw his mother again until he was 41, when Caterina came and visited him and soon after died (Freud, 1910c). However, if his mother was a peasant girl, we could expect her to have breast fed him.[10] Leonardo's drawing of the Virgin and Saint Anne has left us with a graphic image of two mothers, but in this case the two mothers are also a mother and her daughter, with a child, the Christ Child, who is both a child of one mother and a grandchild to the other. These thought-provoking images of two mothers are confusing, not only because they look the same age but also because Mary sits between her mother's knees with their bodies entwined and their feet sketchily drawn. Freud suggested the picture was 'not entirely uncon-strained' (p. 112) which is an interesting way of describing the drawing. He added, as though by explanation, that it contains 'the synthesis of the history of his [Leonardo's] childhood' (p. 112).

When Groddeck (see Chapter 5) expressed his psychic confusion at having a mother, whom he loved and whom he had known intimately in the womb, as well as having a wet nurse, whose warmth and whose breast had nourished him, he was bringing to our attention a child-caring profession that can lead to lasting psychic confusion in the child who has the experience of two mothers. This is a confusion depicted in the Leonardo drawing of the Virgin and Child with Saint Anne and the Infant Saint John the Baptist. Does the child of today, who is seldom fed by a wet nurse, but whose primary caretaker might be a nanny with a bottle, find itself psychologically strung between two mothers? The 20-year research by Hardin (see Chapter 5) suggests that if a child's principal caretaker is a wet nurse or a nanny, when they leave, the child will suffer depression at her loss. Historically the loss of the wet nurse has been more dramatic as she would leave at weaning and the child might never see her again. The loss of the nanny might be expected to be more gradual and the experience of being fed with a bottle would necessarily be less intense and intimate. But whichever method is chosen, if a child is brought up, primarily, by someone other than the mother, they are going to suffer loss when the relationship comes to an end.

Today, with the insights from attachment theory and neurology, therapists are pointing towards the best conditions that can facilitate the development of emotional resilience in the child through understanding the way the infant brain matures (Gerhardt, 2004). One salient point that is being made is that the infant flourishes best in a relationship with a constant caretaker during the early years of its life. In other words, if your caretaker is a wet nurse or a nanny with a bottle, what matters is that she should stay with you until you are psychically mature enough to manage her loss. Such a view does suggest that the mother is the best caretaker, both psychologically and ideologically, unless she is too stressed or depressed, for at the very least, she usually stays with the child throughout its life. This raises difficulties in today's society as mothers need to work to earn enough money to put food on the table. They are also under considerable political pressure to return to work in order to contribute to the economic welfare of the country. This is not all: the latest research suggests that breast milk is best for the baby, for it not only helps to build up the infant's immune system, but being fed at the breast of the mother regulates 'the heart rate and blood pressure' of the infant (Gerhardt, 2004: p. 23). How can mothers manage all these competing pressures when we no longer live in a society with an extended family to help with child-care? The social and emotional demands are intolerable and the debate between those who stay at home to look after their child and those who are either forced economically to return to work, or who prefer to work, are often raucous and punitively self-justifying. One way out of these intolerable pressures is to view the argument that maternal care is best for the child as an 'underground war' being waged by attachment theorists who imprison women yet again with 'burdensome maternal responsibilities', while ignoring a woman's right to 'personal fulfillment' (Badinter, 2010: p. 2).

This may be seen as a powerful feminist challenge to the argument of this book. However the central concern has not been to cast judgement upon mothers who delegate their mothering but to ask why there has been such little psychological or social interest in the way the 'burdensome maternal responsibilities' have been shared, throughout the ages, by the employment of a second mother. It is as though the figure of the nurse, who in fact can only be illuminated against the backdrop of patterns of maternal care, must be air-brushed out of our social history. And this social ostracism in turn upholds an ideological belief that the mother should always be present. One consequence has been an idealisation of the maternal presence followed by a more silent judgement that all mothers should stay at home and bring up their children. But there can be another way of thinking about the problem of child-care that all mothers face when they have a baby. If a mother decides to employ a nanny or put the child into a crèche, the child will make attachments that need valuing and nurturing if the child is to flourish. In such cases the caretaker, because of the delicacy of the infant's emotional development, must be respected. This re-valuing of the delegated mother might in turn lead to a renewed interest in her historical contribution to the way child-care has been arranged across the centuries. It might also mean she was rewritten back into our history books. But more significantly, if she is properly remembered, this may help today's mothers to realise how important the choice of a caretaker for their child needs to be. As we have seen, the loss of the caretaker can create a psychological crisis in the child, if there is a sudden break in this attachment. This can leave the child with an unremembered 'impression' of her presence, as in the case of Freud, and a more silent melancholia, confusion and a crisis in sexual identity and desire. This is not to say that no mother should employ a nanny or that all mothers should stay at home.

And so in conclusion, the nurse has been difficult to discover. She may have lain unrecorded because the relationship between nurse and child came to an end before memory was laid down. However that does not mean her shadow has not lingered in the psyche of the child she has nursed. Her traces can be found in the lives of such people as Talleyrand and Rousseau, where she was an ambivalent presence who clouded the caretaking of their own children. The disregard of the nurse also has historic origins. In the earliest societies she was a slave and though this changed in early medieval Europe, nevertheless prejudices about her class and race and her lack of economic power lingered on and served to diminish her significance. The literary texts of Shakespeare, Dickens and Moore, as well as in the more searing examples of the black nurse in a dominantly white culture, highlighted her lack of social status.

What has also complicated the picture of the nurse's place in our social history is that because she is only reflected in the space that is created by maternal absence, it has been extraordinarily difficult to approach delegated mothering without being caught up in moral judgements. This is well exemplified in Rousseau's self-castigation.

Neither poverty nor labors nor other people's judgment can exempt him from nourishing his children and bringing them up himself. Readers, you can believe me. I predict that anyone who has a heart and neglects such sacred duties will weep long and bitterly for his error, and will never be consoled.

(Rousseau, 1762: pp. 262–3)

But, as we have seen, Rousseau's belief in the sacredness of nourishing his own children only came to him after he had put them into a foundling hospital. Against that ideal of the sacred duties of parents there have always been political, social, economic and psychological reasons that have accompanied the employment of a 'second mother', such as the death of Rousseau's mother at his birth. All these factors have been important in understanding the psychological and social neglect of the nurse.

The combination of historical texts on child-care, such as Fildes' (1988), Boswell's (1988) and Gaythorne-Hardy's (1988) as well as the use of literary descriptions and biographical accounts, which have been put alongside recent research on attachment and neurology, allow a new appreciation of the crucial importance that should be given to present day child-care arrangements. These texts have helped to bring to life the conflicts that have surrounded the history of child-care, but they also highlight the importance of the early years of childhood. They bring to our attention the realisation that these early years are the formative grounds upon which a good society is built. There are many parents today who do not have the economic luxury of being able to bring up their children themselves, while there are others who prefer to delegate their mothering. But whatever the circumstances, there are psychological difficulties that can accompany delegated mothering, if it is not well handled. This knowledge needs to be openly discussed and widely disseminated so that parents may be in a better position to re-evaluate the competing demands of work and child-care.[11]

Notes

1. Others include Davies (2001); Kandel (1999); Olds and Cooper (1997); Pally (1997); Panksepp (1998); Schore (2002); Solms (1996); Stern *et al.* (1998); Tutte (2004); Westen (1999).
2. Fakhry Davids (2011) in *Internal Racism* and Barbara Fletchman Smith (2000, 2011) in *Mental Slavery: Psychoanalytic Studies of Caribbean People* and *Transcending the Legacy of Slavery. A Psychoanalytic View* have addressed more generally the legacy of racism upon psychoanalytic practice.
3. I am indebted to Melanie Hart for her comment.
4. It is interesting to note that in a recent biography of Martha Freud there is no mention of the employment of wet nurses. They may have been employed for all her children except Anna, who was fed by a bottle. This is a good example of what one finds in many biographies – wet nurses are seldom mentioned because they are not thought to be significant.
5. And yet Freud was to write, 'A mother's love for the infant she suckles and cares for is something far more profound than her later affection for the grown child' (Freud, 1910c: p. 117).

6. George Lakoff has described these two views, or 'frames' as 'the strict-father model' versus the 'nurturant-progressive model'. The history of these divergent views he maintains 'goes back to the Bible ... the strict father God and the nurturing God' (Interview. *Guardian*, 1 February 2014). Similarly Gerhardt (2004) contrasts those who take the view that 'what matters is a culture of empathy' that is 'passed on from parents to children' against the view exemplified by Steven Pinker (2002), who does not believe that the way one is treated in childhood is passed on to the next generation, instead he 'advocates punishment to keep people in line' (p. 179).

7. In 1532 Erasmus wrote to the Bishop of Vienna, John Faber, about Thomas More: 'he lives happily with his family, consisting of his wife, his son and daughter-in-law, three daughters with their husbands and already eleven grandchildren. It would be difficult to find a man more fond of children than he' (quoted in Reynolds, 1965: p. 214).

8. A hundred years later, when Puritanism had become the dominant moral training for the young, John Wesley's mother, Susanna, wrote, 'In order to form the minds of the children, the first thing to be done is to conquer their will, and to bring them to obedient temper' (quoted in Pinchbeck and Hewitt, 1969: p. 274).

9. In the 1888 edition of Mrs Beeton's *Book of Household Management*, the reader is exhorted to remember that though servants are essential to the good running of the household, they need to be watched: 'the sensible mistress takes lunch with the children, in order to guard against their picking up "many little vulgar habits from their nurse"' (quoted in Hughes, 2006: pp. 390–1).

10. Freud (1910c) interprets a memory that Leonardo recorded in his notebooks: 'while I was in my cradle a vulture came down to me, and opened my mouth with its tail, and struck me many times with its tail against my lips' (p. 82). This was a phantasy taken from his 'suckling period' (p. 82), the vulture being his mother, who had kissed him passionately on the lips.

11. A recent research report by the Sutton Trust concluded that the bond between mother and child 'from birth to the age of three is even more crucial to a child's development than poverty and other disadvantages', but in cases where the mothers were working, the bond between mother and child was not necessarily broken if there was good quality 'alternative care' (*Guardian*, 21 March 2014).

References

Ackroyd, P. (1999) *The Life of Thomas More*. London: Vintage Books.

Badinter, E. (1981) *Mother Love: Myth and Reality – Motherhood in Modern History*. New York: Macmillan.

Badinter, E. (2010) *The Conflict: How Modern Motherhood Undermines the Status of Women*. New York: Metropolitan Books; Henry Holt & Co.

Behling, K. (2005) *Martha Freud: A Biography*. London: Polity Press.

Boswell, J. (1988) *The Kindness of Strangers: The Abandonment of Children in Western Europe from Later Antiquity to the Renaissance*. London: Penguin.

Bowlby, J. (1973) *Attachment*, Vol. 11. London: Hogarth Press.

Carpenter, M. (2009) *Reformatory Schools, the Children of the Perishing and Dangerous Classes, and Juvenile Offenders*. London: General Books. (First published in 1851 by C. Gilpin).

Clyman, H.G. (1991) The procedural organization of emotions: a contribution from cognitive science to the psychoanalytic theory of therapeutic action. *Journal of American Psychoanalytic Association* 39: 349–82.

Cunningham, H. (2006) *The Invention of Childhood*. London: BBC Books.

Davids, F.M. (2011) *Internal Racism. A Psychoanalytic Approach to Race and Difference*. London: Palgrave Macmillan.

Davies, J.T. (2001). Declarative and non-declarative memory. *International Journal of Psychoanalysis* 88(3): 449–63.

Fildes, V. (1988) *Wet Nursing: A History from Antiquity to the Present*. Oxford: Basil Blackwell.

Fletcher, A. (2008) *Growing Up in England: The Experience of Childhood, 1600–1914*. New Haven; London: Yale University Press.

Fletchman Smith, B. (2000) *Mental Slavery: Psychoanalytic Studies of Caribbean People*. London: Karnac.

Fletchman Smith, B. (2011) *Transcending the Legacy of Slavery: A Psychoanalytic View*. London: Karnac.

Freud, S. (1910c) *Leonardo da Vinci and a Memory of his Childhood*. S.E.11. London: Hogarth Press.

Freud, S. (1926d) *Inhibitions, Symptoms and Anxiety*. S.E.20. London: Hogarth Press.

Freud, S. (1961) *Letters of Sigmund Freud. 1873–1939*, E.L. Freud (ed.), T. Stern and J. Stern (trans.). London: Hogarth Press.

Gaythorne-Hardy, J. (1988) *The Rise and Fall of the British Nanny*. London: Weidenfeld & Nicolson.

Gellius, A. (2012) *The Attic Nights of Aulus Gellius*, Vol. 2, Rev. W. Belloe (trans.). Forgotten Books. www.forgottenbooks.org.

Gerhardt, S. (2004) *Why Love Matters: How Affection Shapes a Baby's Brain*. London; New York: Routledge.

Grinberg, L. (1997) Is the transference feared by the psychoanalyst? *International Journal of Psychoanalysis* 78(1): 1.15.

Hochschild, A.R. (2003) Love and gold. In: *Global Woman: Nannie, Maids, and Sex Workers in the New Economy*, B. Ehrenreich and A.R. Hochschild (eds). London: Granta Books.

Hughes, K. (2006) *The Short Life and Long Times of Mrs Beeton*. London: Harper Perennial.

Kandel, E.R. (1999) Biology and the future of psychoanalysis: a new intellectual framework for psychiatry revisted. *American Journal of Psychiatry* 156: 505–24.

Klapisch-Zuber, C. (1987) *Women, Family and Ritual in Renaissance Italy*. Chicago; London: Chicago University Press.

Manton, J. (1976) *Mary Carpenter and the Children of the Streets*. London: Heinemann.

McLaughlin, M. (1976) Survivors and surrogates: children and parents from the ninth to the thirteenth century. In: *Centuries of Childhood*, L. deMause (ed.). London: Souvenir Press.

Moore, G. (1894) [1999] *Esther Waters*. Oxford: Oxford World Classics.

Olds, D. and Cooper, A.M. (1997) Dialogue with other sciences: opportunities for mutual gain. *International Journal for Psychoanalysis* 78(2): 219–27.

Pally, R. (1997) Memory: brain systems that link past, present and future. *International Journal of Psychoanalysis* 78(6): 1223–35.

Panksepp, J. (1998) *Affective Neuroscience: The Foundation of Human and Animal Emotions*. New York: Oxford University Press.

Pinchbeck, I. and Hewitt, M. (1969) *Children in English Society. Vol. 1: From Tudor Times to the Eighteenth Century.* London: Routledge & Kegan Paul.

Pinker, S. (2002) *The Blank Slate.* Harmondsworth: Penguin Allen Lane.

Reynolds, E.E. (1965) *Thomas More and Erasmus.* London: Burns & Oates.

Ross, J.B. (1976) The middle-class child in urban Italy, fourteenth to early sixteenth century. In: *The History of Childhood,* L. deMause (ed.). London: Souvenir Press.

Rousseau, J.-J. (1762) *Emile,* P.D. Jimack (trans.). London: Everyman; J.M. Dent.

Russell, P.L. (2006) Trauma, repetition, and affect. *Contemporary Psychoanalysis* 42: 601–20.

Sandel, M. (2012) *What Money Can't Buy. The Moral Limits of Markets.* London: Penguin Books.

Schore, A.N. (2002) Advances in neuropsychoanalysis, attachment theory, and trauma research: implications for self psychology. *Psychoanalytic Inquiry* 22: 433–84.

Shorter, E. (1977) *The Making of the Modern Family.* New York: Basic Books.

Solms, M. (1996) Towards an anatomy of the unconscious. *Journal of Clinical Psychoanalysis* 5: 331–67.

Stern, D.N, Sander, L.W., Nahum, J.P., Harrison, A.M., Lyons-Ruth, K., Morgan, A.C., Bruschweiler-Stern, N. and Tronick, E.Z. (1998) Non-interpretive mechanisms in psychoanalytic psychotherapy: the 'something more' than interpretation. *International Journal of Psychoanalysis* 79: 903–21.

Suchet, M. (2004) A relational encounter with race. *Psychoanalytic Dialogues* 14: 423–38.

Suchet, M. (2007) Unravelling whiteness. *Psychoanalytic Dialogue* 17: 667–886.

Tucker, M.J. (1974) The child as beginning and end: fifteenth and sixteenth century English childhood. In: *The History of Childhood,* L. deMause (ed.). London: Souvenir Press.

Tutte, J.C. (2004) The concept of psychical trauma: a bridge in interdisciplinary space. *International Journal of Psychoanalysis* 85(4): 897–923.

Weiskrantz, L. (1997) Memories of abuse, or abuse of memories? In: *Recovered Memories of Abuse: True or False?* J. Sandler and P. Fonagy (eds). London: Karnac Books.

Westen, D. (1999) The scientific status of unconscious processes: is Freud really dead? *Journal of American Psychoanalytic Association* 47: 1061–106.

Winnicott, D.W. (1978) *Through Pediatrics to Psychoanalysis.* London: Hogarth Press.

Young-Bruehl, E. (2012) *Childism: Confronting Prejudice Against Children.* New Haven; London: Yale University Press.

Index